CH00871734

LIZ

LIZ

THE LIFE OF ELIZABETH SARAH CRUSE JACOBS

ELIZABETH JACOBS

To order additional copies of this book, contact:
Xlibris
844-714-8691
www.Xlibris.com
Orders@Xlibris.com
816569

CONTENTS

Foreword

I want to clarify that my intention is not to destroy anyone, but I pray that this book will help others overcome. People who have known my family and me may know some of the people in this book, and I ask that you not judge them as we all change over time. I do not want to cause harm on someone who has changed for the good and cause them to regress in their growth. As a result, there are no names mentioned.

I have chosen to forgive those who have caused me pain and to walk in the freedom that God desires for us to walk in. Only forgiving those who have hurt and offended us will allow us to walk in this freedom.

Many times, I have said I will not wish my life on my own worst enemy, but I am glad I have been able to live it. Because I and my children have gone through so many things, it allows me to minister to almost everyone. I can understand their pain and relate to what they are feeling because, in most cases, I have also gone through it.

I have argued with God for a number of years about writing this book, but He wouldn't release me to do any more writing until I completed this. It is my prayer that by my sharing, I can help someone walk in victory and become what God wants them to be. If this book can make a difference in one person's life, it will be worth the pain of reliving the past.

For many years, my childhood was blocked out of my mind. As God has been healing me of my past, He has been revealing those things to me. He is always so good and reveals them to you when you are ready to deal with each memory so healing can be a reality.

Acknowledgments

Special thanks to the following:

- Mary Tournai for proofreading and the walking talks as this was coming together;
- Lure Voelkelt for the encouragement and prayer;
- Kawika Cornelius for his spiritual encouragement and emotional healing and also for being my accountability partner to keep me on track with the Lord.
- The late Pastor Luree Tatum, my spiritual mother, who always seemed to know where I need a breakthrough and whose discernment and deliverance ministry was so used by God to help the healing process;
- my Freedom and Joy family, who has always been so encouraging and loving, for having faith in the calling God has on my life;
- J. R. Morgan, the first one to prophesy over me that God has a book for me to write;
- the many friends who kept telling me I needed to write about my life;
- my longtime friend Glenda Johnson, who always makes sure I get out and don't hibernate or focus on nothing but work and also has many times been my shoulder to cry on;
- my spiritual father and his wife, the late reverend Bill Beard and his beautiful wife, Terry Beard, who didn't know what God was taking me into but knew my heart and trusted me as I stepped out in new things in the Lord.

Introduction

I pray that by telling my story, I am able to help someone in their Christian walk. I have avoided mentioning names as my intent is not to destroy anyone. People do change over the years, and I do not want to destroy someone who has changed for the better. The people who know me will probably be able to figure out who the people in this book are. This is not to expose them or destroy them.

I had felt that God was telling me to write this for quite some time and kept trying to ignore it. Prophets prophesied that I would be writing, and other people, out of the blue, would say I needed to write a book as it would help so many people. As many Christians can understand when one drag one's feet, God finally put me in a place where I was ready to do what He wanted and revisit the pain of the past. I had also included things that I felt were unique points of interest and some things that were maybe a little humorous.

I realize that some of the things I mention may be very transparent. I had argued with God about it as I really didn't want to tell some of them. He informed me that if I left them out, the people He wanted ministered to would not get the ministry He wanted. As a result, I did as He wanted.

I had revisited the past many times while ministering to someone one on one, particularly in Africa. I had started a couple of other books that I kept arguing with God about writing as they would be more fun to write, but I just couldn't seem to move on with them and have now chosen to quit fighting God and do as He wants, and then I know the others will follow.

You may wonder why some things are included, but please read on as, eventually, it will all come together. In the areas where I talk about the Jezebel spirit, please remember that people can be good Christians and may still operate under a Jezebel spirit. The public may see a totally different person from the one in the environment. That is the reason it is so important to check your heart and your motives.

I had tried my best to put things in the order they happened, but in some areas, I was being hit with so much stuff that I am not sure of the order that it was happening. I know that they happened, and with those things, I put them as God reminded me of them so they can be an encouragement to you when the ending miracle or breakthrough is revealed.

Also, I want to mention the importance of not becoming bitter over what we have gone through. For many years, I was deceived that God really didn't care about me and what I was going through, and I wondered where He was. I have come to realize that He was there and that those things hurt Him very deeply. I realize many things could have turned out far worse than they did hadn't He been there, protecting and taking care of me.

Chapter 1

My mother was at the hospital, waiting for me to come. She had gone in a week early as there was a blizzard forecast for the week I was due, and she had an hour of labor on her previous pregnancy. They wanted to make sure she made it to the hospital to have me. They induced labor, and I refused to come, so they finally sent her home. A week later on a bright sunny day on February 7, 1948, I decided to come into this world without any complications. I never did hear how long she was in labor with me. All I ever heard was I refused to come on the day they wanted, and she missed all her beauty clients twice because I refused to be born early.

They named me Elizabeth Sarah, after both of my grandmothers. My mother decided I was to be called Beth as they always called her mother Lizzie, and she hated that nickname.

I was told I was a very cranky baby. Mom said whenever she would hold me, I would cry. My dad could take me and just gently put me up and down, and I would be content. I had not been told much about those years other than that when I was big enough to walk, my elder brother, who was eighteen months older than me, and I would wander around the neighborhood. I am sure the neighbors were really excited about that as I was told we would pick their flowers and take them to the couple on the opposite corner who had adopted us as their niece and nephew.

I did have an eldest brother whom most people weren't aware of as he was nineteen years older than I was, and he was going to college at the time I was born. He was from a previous marriage of my mother as she was widowed shortly after he was born.

When I think about where we lived and what could have happened to us, I cringe. To the east of our house/beauty shop was a very busy filling station, a north-south highway, and railroad tracks. It was fairly close to the railroad station, and there were a lot of trains in and out of the station during that time. I know God had to have been watching over us that nothing happened to us.

My dad had a restaurant at the east end of town. I was told it had been very successful until his first wife passed away, and after that, it started going downhill until he finally lost it. It was also my understanding that he had been studying for the ministry when my mother met him, and she said she had always wanted to be a minister's wife. I don't know why he never continued with it as no one ever told me.

After he lost the restaurant, we moved back to the area where my parents were raised and lived in my grandmother's house. She had a small apartment in front of her house with a bathroom we shared with my uncle who lived with my Grandmother. The kitchen/living room became the beauty shop, and we all shared one bedroom. My brother and I slept on bunk beds, and I slept on the top bunk.

I would scream at my mom because my uncle was always opening the bathroom door on me when I was bathing or going to the bathroom. She would get after me, saying it was an accident and that he really didn't mean to. I don't remember if they ever put a lock on it or not, but it does seem to me like my father did finally put one on.

My grandmother also owned the little house to the east of her house that she had rented out, another small rental house to the west, and some farm ground that the Republican River ran through. The land later was divided so they could put the highway through. The neighbors to the east suddenly moved, saying they had gotten a job in the capital city, so we moved into the little house, and my grandmother consented to sell it to us.

It seemed like I was always in trouble, and most of the time, I didn't know what I had done. Most of my life when I would make a mistake, I would see myself sitting on a bench outside my grandmother's house, with my uncle standing over me with his fist doubled up, yelling at me, "Your mother deserves a better child than you! You are so bad, and you can't do anything right!" and things like that. I always wished I knew what I had done so I could be a good kid.

The girl who had lived next door, just before she died, called me, telling me that she and my brother would lie about what they had done and would blame it on me so they wouldn't get in trouble. The piece of that puzzle had finally come together. She apologized for the pain she had caused me. My brother says he doesn't remember it. I was in my late sixties when I got the call. I really wasn't a bad kid. I wasn't the perfect child, but I always wanted to do what I was told as I didn't want to get in trouble.

The house was about twenty-four square feet. Mom had her beauty shop in the living room; we had a kitchen and still shared the bedroom. The kitchen was also shared with whatever livestock we might be raising at the time. Over the years, we hatched ducks and geese and had rejected lambs and baby chickens that weren't doing well in our small kitchen.

We raised chickens in Grandma's barn for many years. To the north of the house was a swamp that Mom eventually had them fill in, and she built a chicken house on it. After the chicken house was built, we had layers and sold eggs at a little place that bought them and shipped them out on the train. We also raised chickens that we dressed and sold in the local grocery store.

Each summer we would put in a truck garden, and my brother and I would sell the vegetables in the neighborhood. Mom would always can the overflow that we couldn't sell, and we would store them in my grandmother's root cellar. The root crops that didn't need canning were also kept in the cellar. One weekend Mom sent my brother and me over to the cellar to get some things for her. We always turned on the light, which was inside Grandma's house, as sometimes we would find snakes down there, and we didn't want to put our hand in to get carrots or potatoes and grab a snake. The area was also known for rattlesnakes, so we always tried to be careful.

This particular day, after we turned the light on and got all the way into the cellar, the light suddenly went out. My brother and I headed for the door, thinking maybe the light had burned out. Before we could get to the door, we saw it shut on us. We tried to push the door open, but it wouldn't open. We started yelling, and finally, we heard our dad ordering my uncle to get off the door and let us out. He refused to get off. I guess my dad must have tried to pull him off as we heard my uncle yell for Dad to get his hands off him. Finally, my brother and I were able to lift the door to see my uncle and my dad in a fistfight. I really don't remember much after that or who won the fight, but I heard how terrible a person my father was that he would fight a handicapped man. (He had polio when he was young and also broken his foot. The foot didn't heal right, but the polio hadn't crippled him much.) We were never asked what had happened.

Another time, my uncle threw my brother's dog into the river and wouldn't let it out. Finally, my brother jumped into the river to try to save his dog, and my uncle tried to hold his head under the water. I kept yelling for help, but we were far enough away from the houses that no one could hear me. Finally, I attacked my uncle and knocked him down so my brother could get out of the river. I don't remember anyone trying to find out what happened; I just remember being told what a terrible child I was.

As soon as my brother and I were big enough, we were required to help with dressing the chickens. When we first started, we were only required to help with the plucking. As we grew older, they started expecting us to help with the cutting up of the ones we kept for ourselves and preparing others for the market. The pastor and his wife would many times join us as Mom always made sure the firstfruits went to the pastor. When the chicks were ordered, they would always send out extra to cover any loss in shipment. God blessed us, and there was seldom any lost in shipment and once we received them.

Then the government decided we could no longer dress the chickens ourselves if we were to sell them in the stores as our equipment wasn't stainless steel. We found some people in a neighboring community who would do it, so we would catch the amount big enough to dress and take them up the night before. The next evening, we would pick them up and take them directly to the store. Then the government told us we could no longer sell them in the store unless we started injecting them with preservatives. I am not sure if this was before or during the dressing process, but my dad said he was not going to have formaldehyde put in them, so our business was ended by government regulations. We did continue to raise chickens, but it was only for private use.

When I was five, my mom took me to the pastor's house. She had taken me there to be prayed for as I was complaining about a lot of pain. The pastor met us outside along the curb and prayed for us. I immediately wanted to get down and play with the neighbors. Mom said that she didn't have time as she had to get back to her customers. Many of her customers were in either the medical field or the educational field, and she was told I was showing signs of polio. That was when there was an epidemic of it. When they started doing vaccines at school, I wanted to take them, but she said no. When I asked if she was concerned about me getting polio, she told me this story. She did finally consent to my getting one, and it made me so sick that I had to come home from school. I never took another one until I started going overseas to minister and then only because they said they had no way of testing to see if I previously had it.

My grandmother owned the car we used, but she let my mother or dad drive most of the time. She owned an Oldsmobile with suicide doors. For anyone who may not know what those are, they are doors that open from the middle. We were coming home from church, and my brother was in a hurry to get out. Whoever was driving slowed down to turn into the driveway. My brother opened the door, and it sucked him right out into the ditch. When we checked the damage, his face was almost like hamburger, and he had pieces of his cheek gaping open. We prayed for him, and when the scab came off, you could see where God had put stitches in his cheek where the skin was gaping open. He did not have one scar from that accident. We give glory to God and want to encourage you not to limit God on how He can heal.

I couldn't understand why none of the neighbor girls were allowed to come over and play. Later, I was to find out that it had to do with my uncle, who lived next door. We only had one girl in the neighborhood, and the rest were boys. As a result, if I had anyone to play with, it was the neighborhood boys. I also spent a lot of time climbing in the hills to the south of the house and climbing trees along the river. Because they did have a free swimming pool close to the house, I did spend quite a bit of time there in the summer and also swimming in the river.

I sat up on a rock one time that had pulled away from the rest of the hill, wondering if Mom ever looked out to see where I was or wondered if I was okay. I had found where I thought a caveman had lived, and it looked like the roof had caved in. I climbed around on the wall. I also went into the caves. There was one I started to go in that had paw prints in it. Something told me not to go any farther, so I turned around and left, but I always wondered what paw print it was.

One night I woke up in the middle of the night and looked into the kitchen. It looked like someone was sitting at the end of the table. I yelled at Mom as I knew no one was supposed to be in the house other than us. Mom got up, looked around, and could not find anything. Mom was very upset with me for disturbing her sleep for nothing. Many years later, I was sitting at a table shaped almost the same, and was praying. God showed me the vision I had seen, and I burst out laughing. He had shown me a vision of me in the future.

Chapter 2

I started school. Many of the schoolteachers had their hair done at my mother's shop. I had been instructed that if I gave any problem at school, I would be in trouble when I arrived home. My first-grade teacher had broken her toe, and the whole class decided to act up. She spanked the whole class and, when she got her hair done that week, told Mom about her bad day. Boy, did I get in trouble.

I wanted to play the accordion, but they were saying I was too small, so they advised that Mom give me piano lessons until I was big enough to hold an accordion. Mother found someone to give me piano lessons, which my brother and I went weekly for. After I had learned the basics, I would have the teacher play the song for me so I would know how it was supposed to sound. I would come back the next week, play it perfectly, and pass the song without ever practicing. Finally, Mom talked to the piano teacher and told her she was being too easy on me as I never practiced, yet I was passing them. The teacher realized I was gifted and could play by ear. From then on, my teacher would not play the songs for me. In fact, she would get out a new song each week and would make me sight-read it while she counted out the timing. I was finally big enough to hold the accordion, so I started lessons with it. Eventually, I decided I liked the piano better and went back to it.

When I was eight years old, my eldest brother got married. I was so excited about the fancy new dress I was getting for the flower girl position in the wedding, but I was a jealous little brat as I didn't like my sister-in-law because I felt she was taking my brother away from me. She was so patient, and we did eventually become best friends.

After my eldest brother was married, my brother and I would be sent to his house while he and his wife were on vacation. It was usually about two weeks at the most, but they were always good to us. When they started having a family, I would be sent up to spend time with them and help my sister-in-law with the boys. The boys were good kids, and I am sure she really didn't need me there. I did babysit some, but I was able to develop a great relationship with her. She was like the elder sister I never had and, because she was seventeen years older than me, was like my mother, and our relationship was that close.

In the afternoons during the summer, before my eldest brother started having a family, my other brother and I would go to the swimming pool as it was free, and it kept us out of Mom's hair. My mother was a deaconess of a very legalistic church, and when they found out we were going to the swimming pool, she got in trouble. I have to say I was a little mouthy and informed her I had been there to swim, but the person who had reported us was obviously there for a different reason. The swimming was resumed.

They also did not believe in women wearing pants, and I was a tomboy. I liked to hike a lot. It was amazing how gentlemanly the guys were when you were hiking in a skirt. I had a hard time doing it, but I was finally able to convince her that it was more modest for me to wear pants rather than a skirt.

I would swim in the summers until, one day, there was an accident when a little boy drowned. He had been an excellent swimmer, and they found him on the bottom of the pool, not breathing. They were not able to revive him after they got him out of the pool. I hadn't realized how much it had traumatized me, but I pretty much quit swimming after that. Unfortunately, what few times I did go swimming after that, something else would happen that added to the trauma. One time my eldest brother, who could lie on the bottom of the pool without moving, thought he was going to play a joke on me and lay down right behind me. I stepped back, almost stepped on him, and panicked. When he realized what was going on, he really felt bad.

This is just a fun memory. My elder brother had broken his leg, which was in a cast. We wanted to go fishing, and finally, Mom gave us permission to fish on the bridge behind us. Neither of us caught a fish, but I caught a leatherback turtle. It had fought hard to get loose, so I must have done some damage to it. My brother was very upset that I caught something and he didn't; after all, he was older. Mom decided she would dress it so we could eat it. She had never dressed one before, and no one around had an idea on how to dress them, so Mom killed it and drained the blood. She did get it dressed, but it turned out to be a female with all kinds of eggs. My brother and I realized the eggs would bounce, so I played jacks with them for the longest time, and the turtle was great tasting also. We were the envy of the kids for our newfound balls to play jacks with. If they hit a jack and the skin was pierced, we would just discard it and got a new one.

I was finally able to get one friend, and we were close for many years. Her mother and my mother were very close. She was the only daughter, and I was an only daughter. Even though my friend was older than me, I was thrilled to finally have someone whom I could do things with. I was usually at her house, or we would go to her grandmother's and ride horses. She also had an uncle who was close to our age and became a very good friend. He would always get the horses for us to ride and spoiled both of us. When we were older, he at one time took an interest in me, but I wasn't interested. Mom was so upset with me, but to me, he was my uncle, and I wanted it to stay that way.

In third grade, I sat next to a girl, and we became good friends. I would occasionally go to her grandmother's to spend time with her. They lived down by the tracks with her in a little house. I don't ever remember meeting her mother, but I also remember her younger brother. I was always brought up in a way that regardless of skin color; we were to get to know people for who they were. I had not even realized that she was darker than I was or that her brother was black. They were my friends, and that was all that mattered.

When I started fourth grade, they weren't there. I asked Mom what happened to them, and she said the townspeople had run them out of town because they were black. There was an old law that said black people couldn't live in that community. I was heartbroken and had tried to locate them but never been able to do it.

In fourth grade, I saw Mom come into the school and walk right past my room, going upstairs. She came down with my best friend and left without even stopping to say anything to me. When I got home, I asked Mom why she had come to get my friend from school. She said she removed my friend from school because there had been an accident, and her youngest brother was dead. He had opened the door of their station wagon as her mother was going up the alley from her work, and he had fallen out. She thought she would back up to get closer to where he fell out and ran over him. That was back in the day of phone operators, and my friend's brother had heard her call me enough that when he wanted to talk to me, he would give the operator our number. To add to the trauma, they asked me to play and sing at his funeral. I had played the song a number of times before I remembered I was supposed to also be singing. For many years, I couldn't hear the song "Jewels" without bursting into tears.

A couple of years later, my friend's family moved to a town about an hour and a half away as her stepfather worked for the state and had been promoted to a position there. Having my friend move was almost like another death to me. I missed her so much.

I'm not sure if it was the same year or later, but there was another accident. It was a Sunday evening, and my brother and I were told to go ahead and go to church. I don't remember if someone came and picked us up or if we walked, but after we got to church, we found there had been an accident, and they didn't know if the little boy was going to live. Our dad was taking a trailer of stuff to the dump. The hitch of the trailer came loose, letting the trailer go into the ditch. The doctor's son was playing in the leaves in the ditch. The hitch hit him on the temple, breaking his skull. We bombarded heaven for his healing. He ended up with a plate in his head, but he fully recovered, and we give God all the glory.

My friend had delivered a paper called *Grit*. It was delivered once a week. At first, my brother took the route, but then he found other things he would rather do, so I inherited it. I would start the route at around nine o'clock, walk up Lincoln

Street, and deliver until I finished on Hale Street. The last customer on Hale Street had a driveway that went straight to the hills. I would climb the hill and come down on the other side to deliver at some houses on South Main. Then I would go down to Fifth Street, deliver to the rest of that side of town, then get down to the north side of town, and finish at around three o'clock at the Blue Bird Café (my last customer), where I would buy myself dinner. I would usually have a chicken fried steak with hash browns and gravy or what they called an El Rancho steak sandwich with hash browns. The El Rancho steak was not like the ones we have now. It was actually a ground steak of lamb, pork, and beef that was breaded in a spicy batter. Then I would go home and try to get the rest of the chores done at home. The money left over I would put in savings, along with the eleven dollars a month I would get because of Dad being on social security.

My uncle had started raising sheep. If there were any lambs born that the ewes wouldn't accept, we would raise them until they were able to make it on their own. That also brought the new excitement of sheep shearing and all that stuff.

One of the daughters of Mom's customer wanted to go out to watch the sheep being sheared. Her mom consented as long as I would make sure she was cared for and didn't get near the sheep or in the way of the men shearing them. The little girl had a heart condition from birth, so they were very protective of her. I promised I would take care of her, and we headed to the barn.

We stood back and were watching them shear the sheep. They finished one buck, and it got loose, heading straight over to us. I immediately got between her and the sheep, and it started butting me. We kept backing up until he had us backed into the corner. All the while, we were yelling for my uncle to come and help us. He just stood back and laughed. Finally, Mom and her mother showed up and got the buck into the area it was supposed to be. Mom had just finished with the hair of the little girl's mother, and they were coming to get us. I was so thankful that nothing happened to the little girl.

A couple of years later, I had a dream that the men were shearing sheep, and they tried to take me with them when they left. In my dream, I was fighting with them and was able to get out of the bus about half a mile away at my neighbors. In my dream, I broke my arm trying to get away.

I came home from school, and here they were. I went out to the barn, and the guys started making remarks about how they would sure like to take me with them. My uncle informed them they could have me as I was no good to the family. When they were on their last sheep, I went and hid under the wood pile. Even though I was afraid there might be a snake under the wood pile, I decided I would be safer there with the chance of a snake than in the barn with the sheep shearers when they left. Mom had used railroad ties to divide her garden, and she would have the ties stacked on ties to keep them off the soil so they wouldn't rot. I was small enough that I could scoot under it, and that was where I hid. They finished up and came out calling for me, but I would not answer. I realized later that, even though things hadn't played out the same as the dream, it was a dream God had given to warn me of the impending danger. When I heard them pull away and knew my uncle was in the house, I crawled out from the wood pile.

When I was around eleven, they found I had a lot of problems with my teeth. They discovered I did not have room for all my teeth, so they decided to pull the baby eyeteeth that had never come out. After they were removed, they discovered that one of the permanent eyeteeth had grown crosswise under my nose. As a result, we started the straightening process. We started out with surgery to uncap the tooth so they could start pulling it into place. Then they put on the braces.

The first orthodontist was really great and understanding. Unfortunately, he passed away, and his associate took over his practice. From then on, my orthodontic experience was a nightmare. I felt he really didn't like the added responsibility and was really cruel. With each appointment, he would tighten my teeth so tight that they would be just starting to tighten up enough so I could eat when I had my next appointment. I said something to him, and he accused me of just being a whiny baby trying to get attention. I was so glad to get my braces off when the time was done. He told my parents that he couldn't straighten them the rest of the way because the roots were tangled. After the braces were removed, I had four more dental surgeries because my wisdom teeth did not come in right. Needless to say, I do not do dentists unless I am desperate.

I found an accordion that I loved. I'm not sure how much it cost, but I had never seen one like it before or since. It was pearlized metallic blue with gold speckled base buttons, sharps, and flats. Mom said if I could carry it, she would get it for me for my birthday. I would pick the accordion and run as far as I could with it and then set it down to get another grip on the handle. Mom did get it for me.

When I went to put my money into savings, they told me the balance was nothing. The week before, the balance had been almost $500. They said to ask Mom where it was. When I got home, I asked Mom, and she said she had pulled it out to purchase the accordion, and then she and Dad would pay the rest of it. I was very disappointed, but I wanted that accordion really bad. I was told many years later it was a man-sized accordian.

My brother and I decided to build a playhouse. Looking back, we could have only walked in and turned around and come out. It wasn't very big; we had asked permission, I believe it was from Dad, and were so happy about our new adventure. We had just gotten the frame up when Mom came out and told us to tear it down as it was a distraction in the yard and didn't look good. We tore it down, but I realize how she could have made it a learning experience for both of us. It could have been moved to the backyard. She had made the table we ate at all the time, and it was very secure, so she could have shown us how to construct a playhouse that looked nice.

During those years, Mom mentioned she wanted to go to a beauty convention but couldn't go. I asked why, and she told me that every time she would try to go someplace, Grandma would get sick, and she was afraid Grandma might die while she was gone. I told her it was just a ploy, and as soon as she was gone, Grandma would be fine. I didn't realize then that I was daring to confront Jezebel spirits and the problems it would cause in the future. Mom did go to the convention, and as soon as Mom was gone, Grandma was fine.

There was one girl who always wanted to bully me in grade school. One day for some reason, she was bullying me, and I challenged her to fight the next day. I don't remember what I told Mom, but she let me stay after school. We met at a filling station to fight. She was quite a bit bigger than I was, but I wasn't going to back down as I was tired of what she was doing to me. I don't remember what it was she was always bullying me about, but I was tired of it. I honestly didn't know what I was going to do as I had never fought with a girl before since I had brothers, and the girls in the neighborhood weren't allowed to play with me. I was pretty much a tomboy anyway, so that was okay with me.

We got to the place we were supposed to fight, and she informed me that she wouldn't fight with me as she was afraid she might ruin my good dress. Even though it was a hand-me-down from my cousin, it was a nice dress. I was disappointed that she wouldn't fight me, but by my standing up against her, it must have been enough to let her know I wouldn't take it anymore as she quit bullying me, and I was glad of that.

A couple of things happened that drastically changed my life when I was around eleven. The things I will mention people may question, but God confirmed one of them in a newsletter on antique furniture concerning the transfer of spirits. One of the things that happened was that an aunt on my father's side passed away in an insane asylum. She had been placed there to protect her against herself as she was suicidal. Because I was her size and we were poor, they sent all her clothes to me. Not knowing what was going on, I was suddenly consumed with trying to end my life. I had no idea what was going on, and even at school, the teachers would see me trying to choke myself and tell me to stop. They didn't realize what was going on, and I don't even know if it concerned them enough to mention it to Mom or not. I realize now those spirits transferred with the clothes.

The second thing was the death of an aunt on my mother's side. She was the only one of the family who treated me as though I had value. I realized later in life that she treated everyone that way, but because of being told I was so bad so much of the time, she was very special to me. She had cancer, and we prayed and believed for her healing. She was starting to show improvement, and I just knew God had healed her, and then God took her home to be with Him. I was later told that because she was so valiant in her death, it opened more doors of ministry in their area than my uncle could ever have opened through their ministry. They were church planters in Utah, and God really blessed the ministry through her. At the time, I couldn't understand why God would take someone from me that was so good to me. I took it as God saying that I was so bad that I didn't deserve to have anything good in my life.

Chapter 3

My mother decided she was going to add onto the house in three directions. I found out later that if she would have done what she wanted, they were going to consider it as a new home, so she decided to settle for doing three sides to start with. I was so excited to finally have my own room. She added a beauty shop, four bedrooms, and a huge playroom/family room.

When Mom started the remodeling, she had a woman who came in to clean every week. One day my mom was complaining about how tough it was financially, and I mouthed off to her about the housekeeper. We decided I should do the house cleaning for the same amount as what she gave the housekeeper. That was not a good decision as the housekeeper was only expected to clean once a week, and I was expected to keep the house clean.

The transition through the remodeling was not easy. I had to fill Mom's big canner cookers with water and carry them from the utility room into the playroom so I could wash the dishes. It was about all I could do to carry them, but somehow I would manage to get them in and on the table to wash the dishes. The utility room had previously been the bedroom.

By this time, I was being required to fix all the meals except the Sunday meals or when we were having company. Grandma would come over wanting me to practice songs with her at the time I needed to be starting dinner. The first time, I went ahead and practiced with Grandma and got in trouble for not having dinner done on time. The next time, I asked Grandma if she could come back at a different time so I could get Mom's dinner fixed. I got in trouble again for being disrespectful to Grandma. I realized then I was in a no-win situation.

During those years, my schedule during school was getting up and getting ready for school. I would come home, do my chores, get the house clean, and fix dinner. Some nights we had church; other nights my brother and I would be playing the accordions for Mom's friends clubs and practicing for the accordion band we were in. Then I would get around to doing my homework. I thought nothing of going to bed after midnight because of trying to get homework done.

I composed my first song and was so thrilled. I begged Mom to come listen to it, and she finally came into the playroom to listen. I played it for her and was informed that I didn't know enough music to write a song. It was many years before I wrote a song again, and then it was after I had all my children.

I would come home and try to talk to Mom about what went on at school or a problem I was having, and she would tell me she didn't have time to listen. I would many times go over to Grandma's house and try to talk with her. One day Grandma said she always prayed for me as I reminded her of her daughter who had died. Nobody would tell me what had happened to that aunt other than she had died when she was around sixteen.

Mom never seemed to be concerned about my grades in school. I always made sure I did my homework and desired to get good grades, but I got one bad grade on my report card, and she didn't seem to care. I always had a grade average I always tried to achieve, but this class I really struggled with. I asked about staying after school to get some extra help, and she wouldn't allow it. I was able to bring the grade up and was pleased about getting the better grade.

Our accordion band was asked to play on TV in a neighboring state. We were so proud of ourselves, and I do feel we did a good job. Television was relatively new at that time, so it was quite a privilege to have that opportunity.

I was getting to the age where my mother and grandmother were starting to express their anger toward my father to me. Since he was gone a lot and if my brother wasn't with him, he was involved in school sports, I caught the greatest deal of that anger. I hadn't realized how controlling they had tried to be toward him until many years later. The pastor preached one day about needing to show affection toward your children. My dad was on the rocking chair in the living room and called me over to sit on his lap. I was repulsed and did not want to do it. I finally did sit on the arm of the chair for a short time; I never remember my father ever mistreating me at that time, so I know that wasn't the reason I felt the way I did. I don't know if it was all the things my mother and grandmother had said about him, the fact he had never shown any affection toward me, or the things my uncle had been doing. To this day, it is not something the Lord has revealed to me. I know if He wants me to know, He will reveal it at the right time.

The biggest complaint they had about my father was that he wasn't supporting my mom the way they thought he should and that he was never home. He was still a traveling salesman during the week, and on weekends, he would come home and work in the truck garden we had. The truck garden did really well in the summer months, except for the year the raccoons stripped the corn field. I don't ever remember my father just sitting around doing nothing even when he was home.

I did graduate from middle school. I really don't remember if any of my family was there to see it or not. I had gotten so used to either walking to my events or being dropped off that I was pretty much used to being at my functions alone.

Chapter 4

I was so excited to be in high school, and one of my first classes passed a sheet around for us to sign our name. I thought this was a prime opportunity to have people start calling me by my middle name, which was what I preferred at that time. I signed the sheet Sarah Cruse. The teacher got the list and was looking down at it to make sure he knew who we all were and suddenly asked, "Who is Sarah Cruse?"

I proudly lifted my hand.

He looked at me and said, "Oh, hi, Beth." I figured that was the end of my ever being called anything but Beth for the rest of my life.

During my high school years, my favorite places to spend with God were sitting in a tree that had a branch stretched across the river. I would sit in that tree, read my Bible, pray, and cry out to God about the heartaches I was experiencing. Another place to recluse was the hills; I had a favorite place where I could climb and sat, watching what was going on at the house. I wondered if Mom was ever concerned about my being okay since I was up there all alone, and I never saw her even go to the window and look out. I climbed a lot of places that were very risky.

After the bedrooms were added, Mom always opened her home to the visiting evangelists and missionaries who were coming through to minister. We never know what God is going to use to prepare us for our future with Him, but I did learn many things that have been beneficial as God has taken me to the nations in my later years of life. One evangelist who stayed with us was from Florida. She many times testified how she used to raise her hand and curse God, but God is so loving and eventually brought her to Him. She and her husband were heavily into the healing ministry. My dad really needed to have some teeth filled, but we didn't have the money to get the dental work done. I don't remember if they called him forward or if he just decided to come forward on his own, but he went forward for God to fill his teeth. God filled them with enamel fillings, which were a rarity at that time. You could not even tell where the cavity had been. Those fillings never had to be replaced in his lifetime.

I have to say I am so glad that even though we have our faults and things we do not do right in the kingdom of God, He knows our hearts. My mother and father were people of prayer, and I was privileged to experience many miracles and healings that many people have never experienced.

In my freshman year in high school, my brother was able to get his driver's license. Being the little sister and the youngest, I always wanted to go with him. He would go to his friend's places, and Mom would tell him to be home by a certain time. I would be begging him to leave so we wouldn't get in trouble. He usually left when he wanted, but when we got home, I was the one who got grounded for not getting home on time. I never could understand that as the only way I could have gotten home on time was to have walked. I still did do a lot of walking, and walking after dark didn't bother me, but his friends were usually not close to the house.

I asked Mom if I could walk downtown on a weekend and was told I couldn't even though I had all the chores done. I did ask her why I couldn't walk down and window-shop. She informed me that only prostitutes walked the streets and that she wasn't having her daughter walk the streets like a prostitute. I never did understand that concept and still don't today. It was a small town, and if I was going to do anything that bad, she would have probably known about it before the thought even crossed my mind.

That year, they combined a number of the schools in the area, so there were many new students. I had always been on the shy side, so after my best friend and her family moved, I didn't really have a close friend. God brought me three new friends through the combining of the schools. It was a highly unlikely friendship as one was unchurched, two were Nazarene, and then there was me from the Assembly of God Church. Back then, the Nazarenes said that anyone who was baptized with the Holy Ghost with the evidence of speaking in tongues were demon possessed. We were friends all through high school, and I thank God for putting them in my path. My mother didn't want me associating with one as her mother was an alcoholic, but I guess you would say I was dishonoring my mom as I did maintain the friendship. My mother and her mother would let her come to my house, and my mom would occasionally let me go to hers.

I loved walking and would walk to as many places as I could at that time. I walked to the ballpark one night, and one of my classmates offered me a ride in his hardtop T-bird convertible. I refused to ride with him. For one, I really didn't want anything to do with men, and the other was I wanted to walk. I don't know if my not wanting anything to do with men had something to do with my uncle or not as I hadn't made the connection of the things he was doing at that time, and God had not revealed to me what was going on. I just know I would always rather babysit than date or be around a man.

A young man started coming to our church, and Mom decided he was really nice. I felt sorry for him as he had had some kind of accident and had been in a coma for a long period. I do admit he was nice looking. He took an interest in me, and Mom thought I should consider dating him. I did as Mom wanted me to and found he was not the Christian he claimed to be. He always wanted to be alone with me, and when we were alone, he would insist we have oral sex. I hated it, but when I would try to refuse, he would threaten me, telling me some of the horrible things that he had done to people and animals that didn't do as he wanted. I kept telling Mom that I didn't want to date him, but she kept insisting. I finally got to the point that I just flat refused to do as she wanted.

In one of the times when I came back from my eldest brother's, I got to the bus station, and there was no one there to meet me. My mother had told me not to associate with the people who worked at the filling station since they were from the wrong side of town. I had found them to be nice, and they treated me good, but I had tried to do as she said. I waited for quite a while, and no one ever showed up. Finally, I called to see if she was going to come get me. She said she had forgotten I was coming in and that she was too busy. I would just have to wait until she was free to pick me up, which would be around the time they closed. If I hadn't had luggage, I would have walked. In fact, I mentioned to her about leaving it there and her picking it up later, which she refused. I waited there until she finally had the time to come get me. From then on, when I would come in from a trip, I always had a fear of no one being there to pick me up. God did give me victory over that fear as I realized it was not healthy to be that fearful.

One summer Mom let me go to spend a couple of weeks with my friend who was like a sister to me at the capital as they had recently moved there. She had arranged for me to ride with some classmates who were going there for a school activity. We were about halfway there when we were informed one of the bridges we needed to cross was closed because of flooding. The road they rerouted us on crossed a bridge that was built in World War II, and the water was clear up to the edge of the bridge. We were questioning why a bridge that old was safer than a more modern bridge but went on with our trip. We got to the city she lived in to find it was flooded. They were able to get me to my friend's, which I was very thankful for.

We sat on my friend's porch, and even though we couldn't see the water, we watched gas tanks exploding and listened to the news. They were telling us to be ready to evacuate as one of the reservoirs was possibly going to burst. If it burst, we would have been gone. God protected us, and the reservoir didn't burst.

I got home, and that night, I went out to give the scraps from the table to the dogs. I looked up, and we had water to the edge of the house. I went running back in, frightened and yelling to Mom that the river was flooded. The dam had broken and flooded that whole area. It was quite a while before I was able to walk through the fear of having two floods in less than three weeks.

Because my brother could now drive, my eldest brother's uncle decided to invite my brother and me to a fly-in breakfast. Mom would only let us go to them when they were in town, and because they were on Sundays, we had to be done and in church. That put my brother and me in touch with the world of airplanes. That uncle also had a pilot license and was instrumental in our being exposed to that world. I was in love.

One day when I was out at the airport with my uncle, he considered us his family, and I told him how badly I wanted to fly. He talked with his friend and asked him to give me my first flight. By then, my uncle could no longer fly for having had a heart attack, so he asked his friend to give me my first ride. The friend consented, and I was so excited to be able to have my first flight. I climbed in the cockpit, his friend informed me that when he was through, I would either love to fly or never fly again.

His friend had been a bomber pilot in World War II, and I was told he was one of the best. He would get the plane right down into the caves where the enemy had stockpiled their supplies, drop the bomb, and pull right out, having hit the target. He was also a commercial spray pilot and had recently contracted to spray sugar beets. The sugar beets required him to get right down between the rows to get the chemical underneath the leaves, and he could do it. Needless to say, it was quite a ride. If it could be done in a small aircraft, we did it. When we landed, my uncle came out to ask how I liked the ride. My response was "When can I fly again?"

My uncle's friend was also the civilian commander of Civil Air Patrol and got us involved with it. My brother was the cadet commander until he went to college, and I also joined. For many years, that was my life so to speak. In May of every year, we would take the cadets to Armed Forces Day at Lowry Air Force Base. I loved the air shows and wanted to learn to fly. I was told that when I turned sixteen, because of my involvement in Civil Air Patrol, I could get a pilot license through the air force, and that became my dream for many years. I couldn't understand it then, but Mom would not let me go to the air force base and stay for the six weeks' training to get my license.

We had a doughnut sale with the Civil Air Patrol. It seems to me like it was so we could purchase a station wagon for our unit. We ended up with orders for 122 dozen doughnuts. We thought we were prepared for it, but we were far from it. We spent the whole day making and delivering doughnuts. Since Dad sold restaurant equipment, he had access to old commercial deep-fat fryers. Even with those, it wasn't enough to get them out as early as we had planned. We did eventually earn enough to get the station wagon.

The community had an emergency catastrophe practice. It seems like the commander had somehow gotten us an old air force ambulance for it. We practiced and practiced on being able to properly transport the mock wounded. The day arrived, and we all gathered together to start our practice. At the end of the day, the professionals even commented that we had done a better job than the professionals, and we were just kids. We were so proud.

Through Civil Air Patrol, I had many great experiences. Our commander arranged for an air force plane to be brought down for us to fly in. The pilot allowed all who wanted to pilot the plane, but I was the only one who took him up on it. (If my brother was not in college, he would have done it.) Once we took off, the pilot turned the controls over to me, and I got to fly it for around two hours. It was a C-47, and you could even see the patched holes from bullets shot at it.

It was after a Civil Air Patrol meeting just after I turned sixteen that another thing happened that also changed my life. By then, I was the cadet commander of the group. The meeting was over, and my girlfriend and I were headed to the car for me to take her to where her mother worked as a nurse. A carload of boys drove up, and they wanted us to ride around with them. There was just something in my spirit that didn't feel good about it. Some of them were considered hot by the schoolgirls. She wanted to go with them, and finally, I told her I would take her to her mom; and if her mom consented, then that was between the two of them.

We went in, and the three of us talked about it. I told them I didn't feel good about it, and we thought we had talked her into not going with them. She said she was going out to tell them that she wasn't going. I stayed back to tell her mother goodbye and went out the door. My friend and their car were gone. I looked around to see the car weaving down the street. I just thought she had changed her mind about going with them and didn't think anything more about it.

I went back in and told her mom she must have changed her mind as she was gone. I don't remember how I found out, but the next day, I found out they had gang-raped her. The word was also out that I was the one they had wanted. When they found out I was the last to see her before they took her and that I was a primary witness, I became a threat to them. I really didn't think I had much to testify about, but evidently, the gang was concerned that I did as word got out they had plans to kill me.

I was so upset with Mom as she would not even lock the doors. She said if it was my time to go, the locked doors wouldn't make a difference. I hadn't realized it, but some of my adult friends had set up a night watch for my safety, and they would drive by about every hour. Since I didn't know what they had done, the traffic was as upsetting to me as Mom's refusal to lock the doors.

I always loved school and didn't want to miss any. The first day after everything started coming down, I went to school. I worked in the library during my study hall, and as I was sitting at the desk, one of the gang members was sitting at a study table in the library. He pulled a knife out of his pocket, opened it up, and started flashing it around. I wasn't sure what to do but did start praying for God to help me. We were of equal distance from the door, which meant he could get there probably just as quick as I could. About that time, the teacher came in and saw what was going on. He told him to put the knife away and get back out into the study hall. I thanked God for protecting me and mentioned it to my mother when I arrived home.

The next day, my mother decided to go to school with me. I was so embarrassed.

She would sit there and crochet next to me in all my classes. After that, they pulled me from all my classes and kept me at home. If I got out of the house at all, they would come with a station wagon and back up to the door, I would get in and lie on the floor until I got to the couple's house that were trying to make sure I was safe. I missed a whole month of school. I was able to keep up with most of the schoolwork but did fall behind in shorthand as that was a subject you need to be in class to keep up on. I didn't fail the class, but it never did me much good since I was too slow to take the dictation.

During that time, my mother made me go down to the jail with her and talk with the gang leader. She talked to him about his need for salvation. That was really not where I wanted to be at that time. The rest of the ones involved were minors, and he was the only adult. The minors did straighten their lives out, and I do thank God for that. The adult, I was also told, did accept Christ while he was serving his time. I really don't remember much about the trial other than he did receive time.

On one of the trips to Boise, Idaho, to my eldest brother's, Mom went with me. We were on the train, and we were the only white people in the car. Mom decided I should sing. I told her no as I couldn't sing as well as black people. She kept insisting, and I kept telling her no. So she started singing. She couldn't carry a tune in a bucket with a lid on it, and I wasn't about to be embarrassed by her singing in a car full of people who were known for being able to sing. I started singing, trying to drown her out, and the whole car joined in. It turned out they were all Christians headed to a camp meeting in a northwestern state. We had a wonderful time singing together for a good share of the trip.

We had a new pastor voted in for the church. The young people really liked the couple, and they really had a devotion to the youth. Financially, he needed to keep his job in a community about two hours away, and he would come home on the weekends to minister. She took care of all the church ministry stuff through the week. She found out I could play the piano and put me on church services. That saved Mom a lot of embarrassment as I could no longer dance when the music came on.

The pastor's wife decided there were enough young people to do an Easter cantata that year. At that time, I had a four-octave voice range, so she would have me sing any of the areas that needed reinforcements as well as play the piano for it. I look back and marvel at how I was able to do it as my music was all scribbled up with bass, soprano, alto, and tenor all through the book, plus the music was very difficult. People said we did a good job, so I guess I must have done well. I give all the glory to God.

Mom had always wanted me to sing for the all-school show, and I really didn't want to. Finally, I told her I would do it if she would get me a gold velvet dress. She made it for me, and I sang "I'd Rather Have Jesus," and the pastor's wife played for me. I was disappointed as Mom was not there to hear me sing when she had wanted me to do it so badly. The excuse was that someone might call wanting to get their hair done.

I was in choir almost every year, and one year I was allowed to go to a contest. The reason I said I was allowed was that I kept bugging the teacher until she finally let me go. The ones who had been selected had parents who could afford to give them voice lessons. I had never had any voice lessons, but I was determined that I was going to show them. I would listen to the instructions she would give them, and when the contest came, I received a score the same as or better than theirs. I have to admit I wanted to rub her nose in it a little, but I was too shy to do something like that.

Mom had taught the junior boys' class in Sunday school for years, and one who had become an adult was killed in an auto accident. He was on his way to work on a country road. If the country roads weren't traveled much, people a lot of times would take the center of the road. This particular morning, there was another car coming from the other direction; and because there was a slight hill, they could not see each other. They said he had a head-on collision, and the former student was killed. I don't remember if the other person was killed or not as I didn't know them.

I had known that this man had not been living for the Lord, and it really concerned me where he would spend eternity. My mother commented that we would never know what he might have said in his last breath. That has been such a comforting statement to me over the years even concerning those who have committed suicide. Only God knows, and we know He is a righteous judge.

I was involved in FHA for one year as it was associated with my homemaking class. We had a dinner at the end of the year, and my parents actually went. My fellow classmates were all coming up and asking me if I knew a certain couple, and I would tell them yes, that they were my parents. It was actually the first time they had been to any of my school events.

Homemaking class was a challenge to me. I knew how to cook, but I had never been taught how to measure anything. The teacher was one who wanted everything to be done precisely, and you could not add any variation. I finally got that down pat, and then she started us on the sewing part. They didn't make patterns like the clothes I wanted. The project at school went pretty well other than the material for the suit coat was very loosely woven. She thought I should trim the seams very close, and I disagreed with her as I didn't want to have it ravel out. She finally allowed me to do it without trimming but gave me a lower grade. That was back in the day when young girls wore pastels, and here I was with a slim bright orange skirt and a multicolored suit coat of orange, red, and brown.

The home project was where I really ran into trouble. I took the sleeves from one pattern and the bodice from another and made a dress of black brocade and puffy cranberry red chiffon sleeves. Then I also made another similar one of cranberry red brocade and puffy white chiffon sleeves. I was informed you were not to take different patterns and combine them but were only to use one pattern.

I wanted to go someplace, and this was after my brother had gone to college. Dad commented that I should be asking him since he was the head of the family. I spewed out all the things my mother and grandmother had been saying about him and let him know I didn't feel he had any right to demand that authority as he was an infidel and hadn't taken care of us the way he should. My dad was usually very mild mannered, but that was the wrong thing to say. I met with the plaster wall a number of times, and my mother just stood and watched. I do admit Dad was strong, but I couldn't believe she wouldn't even try to stand up for me. I do have to admit my own guilt in it as I should not have mouthed off to him and shown the disrespect like I did. He really wasn't an infidel and he did have a great love for God.

A couple of weeks after that, we were to take the Civil Air Patrol cadets to Armed Forces Day. Even though I had a driver's license, they were not going to allow me to drive. It seemed to me like it had something to do with insurance. My brother was supposed to drive, and we were to leave early in the morning. He had decided to go out on a date that night, and the woman he was dating would always be out very late. He had recently had an accident because he had fallen asleep at the wheel, so I flat informed him that if he was going out, he would not be taking my cadets to the Armed Forces Day event as I did not want to chance him going to sleep.

We got to fighting, and he grabbed my hair. I bit him, and he hit me on the side of the head that had met with the plaster wall. The hit dazed me. Mom stepped over me to go see if he was okay. He says she checked on me first, but I don't remember it. I lay on the floor dazed as she stepped over me. I finally was able to get up and made it to my bed, where I lay and cried silently but realized that was making my head hurt more, so I just kept it all in.

I still had flying in my blood and wanted to become an airline stewardess. Back then, to become a stewardess, you had to be at least five feet two inches and weight appropriate, and you couldn't wear glasses. I had found a place, taken all the schooling, and passed all the classes. There was only one problem. Even though our family had a history of a second growth, I wasn't one that inherited that gene. I had stopped growing at five feet. They offered me other jobs on the ground, but I wasn't interested.

Since I couldn't see that dream fulfilled, I decided I wanted to go into air rescue in the Air Force. This was during the Vietnam era, and they would not let me go in without my parents' signature since my brother was in Vietnam. My parents wouldn't sign, so I had to give up on that option.

My parents divorced the last year of my high school. Mom blamed me for the divorce, but the only part I was to blame for was she was complaining about him and said the only reason she was staying with him was us kids being at home. I mouthed off and told her if she wanted to leave him, she should do it. She didn't need to stay with him because of me.

I finally graduated from school. I hadn't made the honor roll society like I had wanted, but I had come close. I asked if they would let me come back to take the classes I had wanted but didn't have time for before I graduated like woodworking and shop. They wouldn't let me, and Mom was saying I needed to be like the other young girls and start looking for a husband.

Chapter 5

I had just graduated from high school and wanted to get a job, but my mother was insistent that I needed to go to my eldest brother's again for the summer. I heard Grandma tell Mom she would help with the finances to get me there but that I was never to come back. The uncle who was responsible for the first airplane ride and his wife were going to Alaska and offered to drop me off at my brother's on their way.

We got to my brother's place, and my sister-in-law needed to go to the grocery store and asked my aunt and me if we would like to come along. We were in the grocery store when my sister-in-law said something to me, and I replied right back to her like sisters do. We continued doing that for a while,. Pretty soon my aunt got me over in a different aisle and said something to the effect that she thought my sister-in-law wasn't being very nice to me and that I was welcome to go on to Alaska with them. I assured my aunt I was fine. I guess she wasn't used to people teasing each other like that. Later, I realized I missed a great opportunity to visit Alaska.

I always loved being there with them as my sister-in-law would do things with me and always included me in everything. That year while I was there, since my brother was teaching computer at the business school, he was granted permission to teach me computer as long as one of the machines was free. Since it was a relatively new field, there wasn't a lot of demand; and at that time, they were big machines. It seemed like there was at least one machine free most of the summer, so I was able to get some good computer training for later in my life.

I finally did get back home and got a job waitressing at a café that was a twenty-four-hour truck stop. My dad once said he would never give anyone a tip unless they deserved it. One day he came in, and I had the privilege of waiting on him, but I was afraid I wasn't going to do a good enough job. When he left, he gave me a $0.50 tip for a $0.25 cup of coffee. I knew I had met his approval on the job I had done.

I actually enjoyed waiting tables ("slinging hash" as they called it in my day).

I met a lot of really nice people and was able to get to know many who before were just acquaintances. There was one who came in regularly who had been a couple of grades behind me and was always harassing me. I would get so irritated at him, but I had been trained well in customer service and knew I had to treat him right. One day he came in strutting some expensive new cowboy boots with gold steel toes. He placed his order, and I brought the salad that he had ordered, which was coleslaw. For some reason, when I went to set it on the table, I hadn't gotten it far enough in, and it fell on the floor. I was so embarrassed. It landed right on the toe of his boot, and of course, the gold toe broke the bowl. I know he thought I had done it on purpose, but I hadn't. He never gave me a problem from then on.

My brother just older than me married the woman he was dating. She was at Mom's one night, and an argument erupted. I don't remember what it was about, but it was between her and me. I finally got so mad that I left the house as I knew I would try to hit her. She had a strong Jezebel spirit and many times was not nice to people who dared to try to keep her from getting her own way. I walked down the road, and I heard this car speeding toward my back. God told me to keep close to the ditch and not look back. When it got past me, I recognized the car as being my brother's. I really felt the Lord hid me that night as when I calmed down and went back to the house, she said she had been looking for me and couldn't find me. At the speed she was driving, had she hit me, it probably would have killed me.

A man came into the café with his friends pretty regularly, and he was a couple of years older than I was. I had said I would not consider dating anyone who was not a Christian. He said he had accepted Christ, and I believed him. He was raised Nazarene and struggled with my beliefs. I thought that if anything developed, I could adapt to their belief system. He asked me out, and because of my work schedule, about all it amounted to was him taking me home from work. He did eventually ask me to marry him, and I consented. My mom was so determined that he was the man she had been praying for. I started to question him as I wasn't seeing any changes. There was always an excuse, but being so naive and young, I believed him.

I made all the dresses for the wedding except mine. I was proud of the flower girl's dress as I had designed it so she had five dresses in one, depending on what parts she wore with it. My mom made my wedding dress from a picture, but I hadn't been able to describe it in a way she totally understood what I was wanting. Even though it didn't turn out quite like I wanted, I was content with it. My mother-in-law-to-be wanted to make the wedding cake and said she had made them before and that they were really beautiful. When I saw the cake, I realized we weren't on the same page on that either. It was nice but not what I was expecting.

I had wanted my eldest brother to give me away as I felt he had been more of a father to me than my actual father, and I was still angry at my father for the beating I had received even though I was the one who triggered it. My brother said that the only way he would do it was if my father refused to do it. I decided if he was going to be a part, then he needed to help with it, so I informed him if he wanted to walk me down the aisle, he would have to pay for the flowers for the wedding. He didn't even blink an eye about it and said he would. I should have realized then that a lot of what my mom and grandmother had told me about my father was what I learned later to call slanted truth. (There was just enough truth that it wasn't a total lie, but it wasn't the whole truth.)

We got married on December 31, 1966. I felt like I needed to run, but since the guests were there, I couldn't disappoint them. Plus, after all, he was the one whom God had for me because Mom said he was. I didn't think to talk to God about it myself. They put me in a small room to wait until the wedding was ready to begin. I was claustrophobic and was having trouble staying in the room. I don't know why I had trouble with small spaces, but that and having anything over my face would bring on panic. I don't know if it had anything to do with something my uncle had done or not, and God hasn't chosen to reveal that to me yet.

We had decided to take our honeymoon in a historic town in Nebraska and take in some of the sites there. About halfway through, he said he needed to go home in case his mother needed anything.

Where he worked, they had an extra property where they ran some of the cattle and consented to let us live there. It was about half a mile from his folks' place, and I was okay with that as his dad was elderly. I loved being out in the country with no phone, no car, and no neighbors. The closest neighbor was about a quarter mile away. We would only go to town on Sundays unless there was something that required our going during the week. We would go to church, get groceries, and come home.

He had two palomino horses when we married. Then his dad let us have the milk cow and had given us two spotted Poland China sows. It was just the dog, the horses, the milk cow, the pigs, and me. We did buy a couple of sows later. The agreement was that my husband was supposed to milk the cow. I had been informed they were supposed to be milked about the same time each day; it would be getting late, and he still wasn't home. So I decided I would go ahead and start, and he could finish when he got home. I had milked my brother's goats, so I thought milking the cow would be a piece of cake. I found I got tired before I was finished, but I did get her milked, so I could do it. It never failed; he would come over the hill just as I let the cow out of the barn. Then instead of him coming home, he would go over to his mother's because he didn't want to offend her.

I did have family come out to see me once. When they came, we had been having trouble with the well and hardly had enough water for the cows. It had just snowed the day before, so there was some mud on the floor, but it wasn't bad. I also had not done the dishes, trying to save water for the cattle. I apologized to them for the house not being as clean as usual and thought they would understand as they had also been raised on the farm. Later, I got word that they had told the family that the house was really dirty. It really hurt as I had always tried to keep a meticulous house.

I tried working at the nursing home where my husband's mother worked but hurt my back, so I had to give up that job. That was back in the day when you had to manually lift the stroke patients and move them. It usually took two people to do it, and it was deadweight. By then, I realized I was pregnant, so I decided to just stay home and give the baby pigs TLC.

We got them up to weaner stage and advertised them for sale. We had someone come and look at them, and they said they thought the price was too high for them even though they were big for their age. All that TLC caused them to grow faster. We came home from church the following Sunday to find all the weaner pigs gone. We went over to my in-laws and called the sheriff. We were informed since we did not have a receipt of purchase for the sows, we could not prove they were ours so they would not investigate it. We had thirty-two pigs that were stolen from us.

It wasn't too long after that my husband came home saying we were moving and that he was no longer working for that farmer. I was never informed why; I just started packing to move. Since we had no place to go, we were going to my mom's until he found another job. I was getting pretty far along in my pregnancy at that time. We were to start moving, and his mom needed him to go to town with her to take care of some business. I was told to go ahead and load the car, and he would be back to help when the business was done. I was furious. I loaded the car as full as I could and went to Mom's. When Mom realized what was going on, she would not let me unload it. Boy, did I get in trouble; some of the boxes I had put in the car took two people to unload. I don't remember how many trips I made, but when he showed up, we were down to the stuff that was too big to put in the car.

He wasn't too long without a job, and I was thankful for that. He found a job at a feedlot in a small community just across the state line. The house was provided with it, and it was close to where my mom lived, so I did not have to change doctors. Since we were out in the country, I would sing while I was working. He came home and told me to quit as I was scaring the cows. I quit singing for years except when I was in church.

During my pregnancy with my first son, I had continuous indigestion. I was continually taking Tums. I did not know they are full of calcium. As a result, when I went to deliver him, his bones wouldn't give, and neither would mine. They were talking about having to do a C-section when he finally did come. I had been told the due date would be around my birth date. Had I thought that, I would have gone to the doctor who delivered me to have him. She was still practicing in my birth town about an hour away, and not only was it unusual to have a female doctor but she was also from Russia. My husband's mother had been saying the baby wasn't his and that I had forced him to marry me. I knew it wasn't the truth as I had never had sex with anyone else. My son looked just like his father minus the glasses, so she could no longer claim that.

Shortly after I had my eldest son, my back started giving me problems again. I went to a chiropractor, and he was able to help me but told me the vertebrae in my back was filling in solid and that by the time I reached forty, I would be in a wheelchair. I was just twenty years old at the time.

My husband worked that job for about three months and quit. I can't say I remember the succession of jobs, but there was quite a stretch of them. He managed to get a farming job there in another neighboring community.

The doctor said to start my son on baby food, and he started having problems with allergies to it. That started another issue with my husband's mom as she kept insisting I needed to leave him with her as I wasn't taking good enough care of him. My husband would never defend me but would just let her continue on. I would go home from visiting her in tears. My mother called the pastor of the church there and asked him to come out and pray for my son. God instantly healed him, and from then on, he could eat anything.

My son was just getting big enough to sit unsupported in a grocery cart. One day I was grocery shopping and reached to get something from the top shelf. I went to put it into the shopping cart, and my baby was gone. It was that fast. I looked up and down the aisle and couldn't see anyone. I know it was God as I immediately ran for the door of the store. In the door of the store, heading out were a number of people with my baby. I ran up to them and grabbed him out of their hands, yelling for them to give me back my baby. From then on, even if he was sitting in the cart, I was holding on to his hand.

The farming job didn't last either. He was a good worker, so I am sure that wasn't the problem. We moved back into the area he was raised.

It seems to me like when we came back, he went to work for his parents, and we found a house close to theirs. I was selling Avon to be able to pay the rent and utilities. He wasn't getting a paycheck that I was aware of from his parents, so things were very tight. The house had been empty for a while, and we found there were beehives in the wall. When I would let my son down to crawl, he would end up getting stung.

I caught the Hong Kong flu and was so sick that I didn't have enough strength to lift my baby out of the crib. I would lean up against the wall to get to the crib and lean on his crib to change his diaper or give him his bottle. The days I felt decent, I would go out and take orders for Avon. My mom had given us eggs and milk. We had potatoes from what we had gathered in the fields.

One day I was talking to his mother on the phone. I don't remember if she called me or I called her to ask her to give some information to my husband. Anyway, she started accusing me of stealing the meat off her table and keeping her from enjoying her grandchild. I had never refused to let her see him, and she would go by our house every time she went to town but would never stop. Between the two accusations, I blew up. I'm not sure what I said as I was so mad that I don't remember, and then I hung up on her.

27

It wasn't very long when I got a call from my mother saying she had called claiming I had threatened to kill her. I really don't think I made that threat, but as I said, I was so mad that I didn't know for sure what I said. It wasn't long after I talked with Mom that she showed up with a friend and a pickup, and they packed all the things and moved me into town. She had not realized how sick I had been. I finished the last deliveries and gave up the Avon route.

I am not sure if my husband quit working for his parents shortly after that, but he did get another job sometime later. I believe it was also for a feedlot. For a while, we lived in a trailer house that was on the feedlot. We contracted with the feedlot to purchase all the calves that were born there, and we would bottle-feed them.

I realized I was pregnant with my second son, and I was still very weak from the Hong Kong flu. I had the calves at my mother's house, and Mom had the space in what had been the chicken house. It was my responsibility to feed them twice a day. We were at my mother's until after I had our second child. His mom was saying this baby wasn't his either. Unfortunately for him, he looked exactly like my grandfather on my dad's side, but I knew our baby was his.

His delivery was also difficult as he decided to be breech. Thankfully, his feet stayed together, so he didn't get hung up, and nothing was broken. I made the mistake of only staying in the hospital with him for thirty-six hours. I was informed when I got to Mom's that I had a week to be able to take on all the responsibilities of taking care of Mom's house and doing the laundry for the house, the beauty shop, and Grandma's house. I got to the house, ate breakfast, and then went shopping for groceries. My husband did take care of the calves for about a week and then turned the responsibility back over to me. Of course, all my mom's customers wanted to see the baby.

Two weeks later, I was at a friend's business, and she asked me how I was doing. I said I was doing fine and burst into tears. She informed me I needed to see a doctor. I told her I would be fine. She kept insisting, and my former boss was there also. Both of them insisted I go, and it seems like someone took me. The doctor said I was both mentally and physically exhausted. As a result, I had converted over to nervous energy, and I wasn't stopping. I wasn't sleeping, and when I would lie down, my mind wasn't stopping. He put me on some medicine and said for me to come back in two weeks unless I didn't improve. He also said because of my condition, I could not hold my baby as he would sense my condition and would become cranky. I sat watching someone else hold my baby and crying because I wanted to hold him so badly.

I was finally hospitalized because I could not get on top of it. My family started saying how weak I was that I was having all these problems. The doctor put me on some pretty heavy medication, which I wasn't happy about. I was instructed not to even get out of bed without calling a nurse. I thought that was a little extreme and tried going to the bathroom without calling for help. I began to wonder if I was even going to make it to the restroom. Needless to say, I did call for help to get back and was chewed out royally for trying to go by myself. They tried to give me a different kind of medicine and also tried taking down the dosage, but when they did, it felt like my insides were going to shake out of my body. They told me the medicines they had to put me on were more addicting than heroin, and I would not be able to go off them cold turkey. I told them I wouldn't take them but was informed I would not leave the hospital unless I took them. I was on such a high dosage that if I took one extra pill above the prescribed amount, it would kill me.

I got home from the hospital with doctor's orders that I was not to do anything except get well. My husband, after I had been home from the hospital about a week, informed me he had found a place to live close to his parents that had property so the calves would have more room to run. I was concerned about my being able to take care of the children in my condition. He informed me that he would take care of them at night if I could take care of them in the day. It was all talk as he was always running to his parents and would come home to go to bed. The baby would start crying in the night, and I couldn't get him calm. I would wake up in the morning to find I had taped his mouth shut or he had bruises on his bottom, and I had no memory of doing it. I felt so guilty, but I couldn't get anyone to help me. I continued being in and out of the hospital until they finally suggested I be put in a mental hospital to see if they could get to the root of the problem.

I thought I finally had someone who cared as the psychiatrist listened to me and seemed to be concerned about me. Then I decided to do the math on what he was charging and concluded I could be concerned about someone if I was getting paid three dollars a minute to listen to them. I did tell him how it bothered me that I was being told I was so weak. He informed me that my problem was that I was too strong. He commented that the ones who broke were the ones who were like a tree, while the others were like grass and just bent with the wind where the tree would not bend.

While in the mental hospital, a person was walking down the hall and was trying to get the attention of the man in front of me. He wasn't responding, so they said, "Hey, little man." The guy put a hole in the wall. I tried to stay away from him as much as possible.

There was a bathroom between my room and the other person's room. We had talked a lot. She was a teenager there because of a bad LSD trip. She said the reason she had been using it was that a psychic had told her she would die in a tragic car accident when she was sixteen, and she couldn't live with the torment it was causing her. One evening I needed to use the bathroom, but the door was locked. I finally got a staff member to come unlock it for me. She just unlocked it and left. I opened the door, and there was blood all over the place. She had attempted suicide. Fortunately, she hadn't been able to succeed, but it really wasn't what I needed at that time. It turned out some of her friends had slipped some more LSD into her, she had a bad trip, and thought that was how to get the bad trips to stop.

Then the family decided I was just doing it because I didn't want the responsibility of the boys. The truth was had it not been for the children, I would have walked out the door of the mental institution, and no one would have ever heard from me again. The doctor told me I had endured so much rejection in my life that it eventually broke me. He said at least I knew the problem, but he didn't have any suggestions on how to deal with it.

After six weeks, I was released to go home. I came home to so much hostility that it was really hard. My father-in-law had been taking care of the calves, and when I came home, he kissed me on the forehead and welcomed me home. He was the only one.

I became really rebellious and decided I was going to do everything that my mother disapproved of. I started wearing micromini skirts and dresses. I tried going to church, and people would walk on the other side of the church rather than shake my hand or talk to me. I know it didn't help that, at the time, people were murdering people and getting off on mental insanity. I would not kill anyone. Another thing that really bothered me was that another woman had a nervous breakdown, and the church was there for her but would not help me at all. I did realize I was a lot further away than she was also.

Then my husband made friends with some people who were in the area hauling beets for beet harvest. They persuaded us to move down along the border. I have to admit I thought it would be good as it would distance us from the control of his mother, and maybe we would have a chance. Even though I was a Christian, I had never been taught to pray and seek God's guidance for things like that. Had I prayed about it, I would probably have known it was not a good decision.

When beet harvest was finished, we were asked by some of the migrants to go back with them. We both agreed to the move. The first place we stayed was the house of his friend's father. It was perfect for us, and I was looking forward to the change and getting to know the customs and things of the area.

One morning my husband left the house before he went to work, saying, "If my friend wants anything, you give it to him." His friend showed up that morning, wanting cigarettes; and since they were on a high shelf, I got up on the chair to get him some. I was reminded by his friend that I was to give him whatever he wanted. I was raped that day. I showered and felt like I couldn't get myself clean. I finally got out of the shower because the boys woke up from their naps. I endured that for a year and a half.

During the time we were in that area, we moved another two times. One place did not have an installed bathroom, just a room petitioned off that would someday be a bathroom. We did not have running water or an outhouse. We would just go out behind the sagebrush to use the bathroom. We used the ice chest for bathing and hauled the water from town.

The other place was in a very small community, and he bought it. That one also had a small rental house on the property. The main house had a large hole in the floor that I tried to keep covered as the kids could have easily fallen through, and when it rained, you needed to have an umbrella in the house to protect you from the rain that was coming in. It had a combination sink and stove, but if the stove was turned on, you would get shocked if you were trying to use the faucet.

My dad was calling me twice a week. He never called, and since I knew he operated in the prophetic even as a non-Christian, I knew he was sensing something was going on. I woke up every morning and cried because I woke up. He would ask how I was doing, but I never could tell him what was going on.

Since it was a very small community, you could walk anywhere you needed to go. I would walk to the post office to get the mail and chat with the postmistress. I didn't know she was also the Assembly of God pastor in the community. Somehow in the course of our conversations, she realized I could play the piano. I am sure she knew all about what was going on, but she kept insisting she needed a piano player for church. Finally, I consented, so I would be at the bar on Saturday night and at church on Sunday, playing the piano. I had never known unconditional love, and I attribute a good share of where I am today to her love.

Then she would give me some music and wanted me to sing it for a special for church service. She also persuaded me to come to her Bible study. Since I had no way of getting there, she asked one of the ladies from the church to pick me up. The woman was so short that she looked through the steering wheel rather than over it, but she was also a very loving, caring, older woman.

One day she came to pick me up for Bible study, and the boys had been a little challenging that day, so I had decided not to go. The time got away from me, and suddenly, here she was to pick us up. I told her I didn't think I was going to go as the boys had been a little unruly, and I didn't have them ready to go. She sat down on my couch, scooted clear to the back, and said, "I guess I will just have to stay here as I promised the pastor I would bring you so I won't show up without you." I got the boys ready as I realized I would either go or have her on my couch for the rest of the afternoon.

During this time, I started developing some health problems. I suddenly lost twenty pounds in a month's time. I went to the doctor to be told it was all in my head. At that time, I didn't have much I could afford to lose, so my hip bones were all protruding out. I jokingly said I didn't realize I had twenty pounds in my head. Later, I found it was due to ovarian cysts that did finally break on their own. Also, I developed a lump on my breast that the doctors were saying was cancerous. With my family having so much cancer, it was considered a pretty sure thing, but most of the cancer in the family started in their forties, and I was still in my early twenties. My husband refused to let me have the surgery, saying I wouldn't be any good for him if they had to remove a breast. I also had a miscarriage that I never told the family about. I wasn't sure if it was my husband's or his friend's.

I have to admit I had mixed emotions about the miscarriage and, because of the situation, did not grieve over the loss until many years later.

In spite of the fact that we were now fourteen hours away from his mother's, he would still run home to his mother every time we turned around. If she wanted him to come, we would head down on Friday night after he got off work, and I would drive all night. Then on Sunday night, I would drive all night so he could be back at work on Monday morning. Many times because of the health issues I was having, I was in such severe pain that I could hardly stand to sit, but I would do it.

One night I heard someone trying to break my front door down. If they tried to come through the back door, it would have been no problem, but the front door was solid wood with a dead bolt. As they were finally leaving, I peeked out of the drapes and saw who it was. It was friends of the person who was continually raping me and also sons of some of our friends.

The next day, I was walking to get mail and past the filling station where my friend's husband worked. The guys were filling up their car with gas. I proceeded to tell my friend's husband what had happened the night before. I included in my conversation that we had a rifle, I knew how to use it, and I could outshoot my brother who had received commendation for accuracy. I acted as though I didn't know it was them who had done it. Within twenty-four hours, they had packed up with their families and moved out of state. Their parents commented to me that they didn't even know they were thinking about moving. What I didn't tell my friend's husband was that the rifle was hanging over the door, which was better than six feet high; I would have had to get on a chair to get it down, and then I still would have to load it. I think I did get the point across that I wasn't going to deal with any of their antics.

The man who was continually raping me persuaded my husband to quit his job and take a couple of migrant trucks to the coast of Virginia to work in the fields. I had always felt that no matter where I was, I would try to adapt to the culture, so I would also be working in the fields. I was to drive the main vehicle with the boys and navigate, with the two trucks following. They said it was a twenty-four-hour drive, and we were to drive straight through. I was doing good and making great time other than I can't tell you where I'm at when I'm driving; I just know where I'm going.

We came across this terribly long bridge, and the other lane was under construction. They had narrowed the four lanes down to two lanes with traffic both ways. As a result, I was meeting these huge trucks in the middle of the night, and there wasn't a lot of clearance. I was getting very tense and realizing I was getting tired. When I got across the bridge, I saw the "Welcome to Mississippi" sign. I realized I had just crossed the Mississippi River, and at its base at that time was a mile across. I decided maybe I should stop and get some rest. We pulled over, and I slept in the car for a couple of hours and woke them up to get going again. We finally made it to our destination after I learned Atlanta, Georgia, was not a fun place to go through during rush hour when you were trying to keep watch on two trucks behind you.

Working in the field, I knew I wasn't keeping up with the other women, but I had never done that kind of work before. I was discovering there was a problem, though, as when I would go back to get a drink of water, the men would quit and follow me. Of course, their women were getting very upset, which I could understand. I wasn't doing anything to encourage them and wouldn't even talk with them while I was getting a drink. As a result, there was a lot of jealousy developing. The day things came to a head, we were at a café with my husband's friend who was drunk. He got upset and started walking down the highway, stumbling all over the place. Even though I had problems with him, I still didn't want him to get hit and possibly killed. He also had a family that would have been hurt, so I went running after him to try to get him to return.

As I was talking with him, he stumbled, and I caught him. Someone from the camp went by, saw us, and went back to the camp, telling they had seen us hugging. We got back to the camp, and everyone was angry at me. I knew it wasn't safe for me to stay, and my husband still wasn't standing up for me about anything. I made the decision that I would go back to my dad's. I was going to take the car, drive as far as the gas would take us, and try to get some kind of work to get enough money to make it farther down the road. I realized it was risky, but staying there was going to be just as risky. He said he wanted to keep the car, so he would drive me back to my dad and stepmother's. The plan was I would stay with them until the work there was finished, and then he would come get me to return to our home.

When the work was done, he did return to pick the boys and me up but got a job in the area close to his mother. Until he found a job, we stayed with my brother for a short time. His wife, as I had mentioned before, had a Jezebel spirit and was always stirring up problems between people. One night we had all been drinking, and my brother and I got into a fight. He hit me, and I walked out the door and went to the park. I found out later the people I was talking to in the park were all druggies, but I felt safer with them than I did in his home. My husband had seen the whole thing and had not tried to protect me. He finally found a job that was eight miles from town, and they would provide a small trailer for us to live in.

By then, my mother had found out about the lump in my breast and was determined that something had to be done about it. I knew we didn't have the money for surgery. One of her customers worked for social services, and once they found out about it, they were also determined that something had to be done. They told me I needed to come into the office, and they could possibly help.

One evening my husband took the boys and went to see his mother but told me I had to stay at the house. They were gone for a long time, which surprised me as he never took the kids with him for anything. They came home and went to bed. A few days later, I woke up in the morning to find $20 on the table with a note saying he couldn't take it any longer, and he was leaving. I had no way of transportation and no phone, only the $20 he had left on the table. By the time he walked out on me, I was twenty-four years old and had caught up with my age in moves.

I called my brother who lived in the same town, only to be informed that my husband was with them and that they couldn't help me. Finally, they said they would take me to Mom's. Within twenty-four hours, I had found a place to live, a job, and a babysitter. The apartment I was able to get into was willing to let me pay part of the deposit with each paycheck along with some toward the rent, so by the time the second month rolled around, I would be able to pay for the whole month. Mom was able to gather up a folding table, some chairs, and some beds. I did have the bare minimum of kitchen utensils as I had them in the camp.

The job was waitressing, and fortunately, I was a good enough waitress that I made good tips. Each day I would walk the boys to the babysitter, walk to work, work my schedule, get the groceries I was going to need for the evening meal and breakfast for the boys, pick them up from the babysitter, and go home. The babysitter was a neighbor who made it nice even though she was pretty much a stranger. Then I found out her children were being mean to the boys, so I had to find a different babysitter.

The rapist was back in the area again as it was harvest time for the sugar beets. He would stop in the place where I worked and was demanding I let him take me to Mexico to be his mistress. I told him I would not even walk out of the building with him. He said if I didn't let him and ever decided to go on with my life, I would be dead.

Then he and my husband started coming around the apartment, terrorizing the babysitter, and stalking me. I talked to the police, and they told me to call them whenever he showed up. I told them I didn't have a phone. They told me to go to the neighbor's, which was the home of the babysitter's parents, and use their phone. I said that was really smart to leave the boys in the house by themselves while I went to call for help. They told me if I locked the door, I would be all right. My thoughts were *And what happens while I am trying to unlock the door if they have evil intentions?* They were absolutely no help.

He also started charging his meals at the restaurant to me. When I got my check and it had all the unauthorized deductions on it, I started questioning why it was so small. They informed me he had been charging his meals and had not paid them., According to law, since eating was needed for life, they could take it out of my check. I blew up and told them I had not made the charges, and if they did it again, I would walk without giving notice. They never did that again, but he did still keep coming in and harassing me.

One evening a friend of his from when we were dating came in. He apologized for not making it over. I was totally puzzled as I hadn't known he was supposed to come over. When I got to questioning him, it was the night my husband had taken the boys to visit his mother and insisted I had to stay home. After more questioning, he confirmed I was being trafficked, which I had suspected for some time. That also explained why I wouldn't be any good to him if I did have breast cancer and had the surgery.

The social services director came in where I was working and asked why I hadn't been in to see if they could help with the surgery. I explained to her what was going on, and she insisted I get in there and apply. It turned out my tips were too much for me to qualify, but she said she would take care of it to make sure I was able to get the surgery.

The manager of the restaurant found out what was going on and he offered to stay at my apartment for protection for the boys and me. I felt I could trust him as he was the brother to my neighbor, and I had known her for a long time. I was actually godmother to one of her sons. When he realized what we ate was dependent on the tips from that day, he did take me to the grocery store and had me get the groceries I needed. Because of my husband and his friend terrorizing her daughter, I needed to find another babysitter where they wouldn't know where the kids were. The manager got one of his nieces to babysit for them, and we would take them to her house in his car. He would also take me to the Laundromat to wash the clothes so I didn't have to walk and carry the clothes anymore.

Mom started putting pressure on me to try to get my husband to take me back and, since I wasn't living to her standard, basically turned her back on me. I couldn't tell her all I had gone through, so she didn't understand. I tried to get someone to pick the boys up for church on Sundays, but no one would because I was working at a bar part time along with the waitressing, and I was living with a man whom I wasn't married to while still married to this other man. I felt bad, but I was doing what I felt like I needed to do at that time to survive.

They were able to get me on with social services so I could have the surgery. The niece who was watching the boys said she would watch them while I was in the hospital, and of course, I would pay her. My mother and my husband's mother both refused to watch them during the surgery. I was dropped off at the hospital and checked myself in. I felt so alone, and to go through something like that with no one there didn't help. The person in the room with me was my neighbor and his sister, and she was to have a hysterectomy. Her husband didn't want her having the hysterectomy, so he was in the room drunk, having all kinds of fits. When I was released from the hospital, the man who was staying with me picked me up and took me to the apartment.

When the biopsy results came back, they informed me they didn't know what it was; but from the tests, they could tell it would eventually turn to cancer. I had lived with the thought of having cancer for so long that being told I didn't have it but would have it caused me to drop into a really deep depression. I was talking to my dad about it when he came to visit, and his response was "You've never done anything normal in your life, so what would make you think your biopsy would be normal?" Now I realize I should have taken it as a compliment of being unique, but I took his comment as degrading and hurtful.

I had been in contact with my pastor friend, who had been so loving and encouraging to get me back in church to see if she would take the boys if something did happen to me. She told me she had some severe health problems and didn't feel she would be able to do it. I had also found where my things were as I had been told they had been put in storage. I definitely wanted them as most of the things we had I had gotten before we were married or were family heirlooms. I had plans to get them with my tax return check until I found out that the storage bill on them was the amount of the tax return. I knew I didn't have enough to go down there, get a truck, bring them home, and pay the storage. In the divorce, I tried to get them and was supposed to get them—one of the cars, $50 a month child support—and he was supposed to pay the lawyer fees. I never got any of it.

Six weeks after my surgery, I was able to go back to work but was limited on the lifting. My first night back to work was election night, and I was scheduled on the floor by myself. Fortunately, the gal I relieved said she would not leave until she had salads and things dished up so I wouldn't have to do so much. Instead of filling the tubs, I would just take what dishes I could back to the kitchen each time I made a trip back there. I was able to hold it down and was very grateful to her.

A couple of weeks later, we had a rush, and there were three of us on the floor, and the other two waitresses weren't able to keep up. They said it was because of having so many people to wait on. I have to say I wasn't very nice about it as they just weren't doing their job, and I let them know I had done it by myself about a week before, and I had just come back from surgery.

I hadn't realized it, but the restaurant owners were running a side business. One night as I was fixing sandwiches for the bar, one of the restaurant customers was at the bar. We started talking, and suddenly, he was trying to get close to me. I asked him to keep his distance, and he informed me he had paid for those services. I told him his tips were for the service I gave him when I was waiting tables and that it did not include anything else.

The owner's mother was there, and she informed me that I had to let him do what he wanted. I told her it wasn't happening and went to get my coat and purse. She wouldn't let me get them, so I walked out of the building without them. It was -20 degrees. I was so cold, but I was not going back in there. Finally, someone came to go in and asked me what I was doing standing out in the cold like that. I told them why I was out there, they told my fiancé, and he came out to start the car for me. I found another job and gave them notice. They said I wasn't that good of a waitress anyway. I had to laugh as I was told they had five people working to cover a shift I usually handled by myself.

My protector, whom I later married, had gotten a new car, and he would pull up while I was working, and there would be a woman sitting on the console. I would ask him about it, and he would say she was just looking over the car. I was so dumb, trusting, and naive at that time. He had asked me to marry him and had given me an engagement ring. His sister warned me that if I married him, I would have nothing but heartbreak ahead of me. I told him what she had said, and he said she was concerned that he would quit helping her financially if he married me. Another woman told me he had proposed to her the week before, and I was told she was just jealous. I found out later that he was the one lying.

The other job I was able to get was at the same building where I first started waiting tables. The man who owned it had been in the business for many years and was known to be one of the best. He offered me more pay than what I was getting at the other place. He said the person I was replacing was going to the place I just quit, and they had told him they were getting more pay. I thought it a little ironic. He really appreciated me and my work skills.

There was one night he forgot there was a game in town and that we would have a lot of customers after the game so hadn't scheduled anyone with me. He told my fiancé he saw them all come in and came out to assist me to find I had menus and water to everyone who came in. He said he realized I had it covered and went back to the kitchen to wait for the orders.

Chapter 6

I don't know what happened, but my fiancé was no longer working as manager, and for a while, he didn't even seem to be looking for a job. I had finally decided if he didn't have a job by a certain date, I was moving on. I knew I was pregnant, and I was going to have to do something. I know I talk in my sleep, so I don't know if I told him or if it just happened, but the day came around, and he had gotten a job in a neighboring town as manager of the VFW. We made plans to move.

My boss wanted me to ride back and forth from work with him as he lived in the community my fiancé had gotten the job in. That would have meant some very long hours, and I felt like I needed to be with the boys. He really hated to lose me. He was trying hard to work something out, but we weren't able accomplish it.

We were able to get a two-bedroom trailer house to live in that was on the edge of town. I would make burritos for the bar and take them down to sell on weekends. One night I was home, and I got a call from my fiancé that he needed me at the bar and to bring the boys. He wouldn't tell me why other than I needed to come right away. I got to the bar, and he said he had gotten a call that my first husband and my sister-in-law were headed to the community we lived in, and the person informing him said they didn't think they had good intentions. We closed the bar when it was time and went home. We checked everything and couldn't see that anything had happened.

The next morning, we had the police knocking at our door. The source had been trying to contact us to make sure the boys and I were okay and couldn't get through. We checked the phone, and there was no dial tone. We went outside, and the line had been cut right at the ground. The police said whoever it was who did it was obviously up to no good, and I believe that source probably saved my life.

Shortly after having the surgery, I became pregnant. I was still working the bar on dance nights and fixing burritos a couple of nights a week for the bar. My pay from working the bar was always given to him, and at that time, he did all the shopping and paying of the bills. My doctor had wanted me to have the baby by C-section, but I refused. Finally, we came to an agreement, if I had any problems, he could deliver the baby by C-section; but otherwise, I would have the baby naturally.

My fiancé's sister needed someone to come help her as she was going to have surgery and needed someone to watch her kids. I went to stay with her and to be there to help her while she was in the hospital. I got home, and the house didn't look like anyone had been there at all. I said something about it down at the bar, and the guys told me my fiancé had spent the whole time I was gone with our bartender. I thought it was just small-town gossip and didn't put much trust in it. Then one day he said she didn't show up for work, and nobody knew where she was.

The day the baby was due, I helped dress 148 chickens at my mother's. I was not having any contractions and felt fine. They were all afraid I would go into labor and not make it to the hospital in time. I actually ended up carrying the baby over by two weeks.

We found a three-bedroom home a week before the baby was born. I had made many of the things that would be needed for the baby when it came, so I was as prepared as I could be. We moved, and I painted the nursery. The night I went into labor, I had tended the bar until closing and restocked the bar. I went home and went to bed. I had not been there very long and had just gotten to sleep when I started dreaming I was on a ship, it had wrecked, and I was drowning. I woke up, and my water had broken. With the place being new and my being so tired, I couldn't remember where the bathroom was. I did finally get awake enough to get there, and then I woke my fiancé up to take me to the hospital. His niece who had babysat the boys in the previous community was staying with us, so we didn't have to be concerned about getting someone to come for the boys.

I got to the hospital, and the doctor told them to not plan on keeping me as I probably wasn't that far along. He examined me and told the nurses to get the delivery room prepped as I was having a baby. An hour later, he announced I had a girl.

The doctor commented it was a sin for someone to have so much hair, with him having so little. Her hair was clear down in her eyes. He said he was going to give her the first haircut. I thought he was actually kidding. I did notice as they whisked her away that she was blue and asked what was wrong that they wouldn't let me see her. The cord had been wrapped around her neck, and they had to get her breathing. When they got her stabilized, they brought her back to me. When I got to my room, I noticed a lock of hair on my gown and asked the nurse where it came from. That was when she told me the doctor had cut her hair in delivery. I stayed in the hospital for twenty-four hours.

Things were relatively calm. The owner of the house decided she wanted to sell it, so we ended up moving again. We found a house that had been converted from a barn. It was really cool the way it had been done.

By this time, my fiancé had gone to work for the rural electric company, and I would meet the delivery trucks and tend the bar until he got off work. One weekend as I was hanging clothes on the line, the bartender who had disappeared showed up. She looked like she had just had a baby and said she needed to speak to my fiancé. I told her he was in the house and to go on in. I don't know what they discussed, but she left, and I never saw her again. I was now pregnant with my fourth child.

My fiancé's sister whose kids I had watched started having problems with her eldest son, and my fiancé said we could try to help them. He got a job and was working, but we were having problems with him not abiding by the rules. One night we came home, and once again, he had disobeyed the rules. We got after him. That particular night, my dad and my stepmother were visiting, so I had him sleeping in the boys' room with them. They came down the next morning with hickeys all over their necks and chests. I was so appalled that I tore into him royally. I didn't think to check anywhere else. I told him to give his boss notice as he was not staying with us. I was being nice to let him have the two weeks to give his boss notice.

The family was very upset with me for sending him back, saying he was just too much for me to handle. The one sister whom I was close friends with asked me what had happened, and I told her. She said "I knew it had to be something more than you not being able to handle him." I don't know if the truth was ever found out and if he got help or not. Later, we would find out he had done more than I had thought.

That fall, I was really tired, so I had curled up in the rocking chair to nurse my son and dropped off to sleep. I woke up and looked at the clock wrong and thought I had missed picking the boys up from school. The position I was in had cut off circulation, so when I jumped up, I just about fell. Fortunately, the piano bench was close, and I was able to lean on it, so I didn't drop the baby. I then looked at the clock again and realized I had looked at it wrong, and they weren't even out of school yet. I was relieved as it gave me time to get the two at home out to the car to go get them. I did end up going to emergency to find out I had a bad sprain. They were saying it was actually worse than if I had broken it, and it would take just as long to heal. I was ordered off my feet as much as possible and to keep it elevated. I dried up instantly and was no longer able to nurse my son, which really bothered me.

A couple of months later, the landlord said he wanted us to move, saying he didn't want people like us in his house and accusing us of being chicken thieves. We told him we had not stolen any chickens and that he could check with the police or even check with my mother as she had raised them and it was where we had gotten them. We had dressed them at her house and brought them home to put in the freezer. He refused to reconsider, so we started looking for a different house. We were hoping to buy so we wouldn't have to be moving so much.

We found one that was for sale in a neighboring town and were told we could move in and pay rent until we could get the loan and process the sale. We moved in, and the house, even though it needed quite a bit of work, was nice. It was a two-story older home; there was also a rental house on the property. We found we weren't able to get a title as there was some kind of problem, but we could still continue to rent the place if we chose to. We chose to stay and continued to look for a home to purchase.

The little house on the property was rented, and the family seemed really nice, but they didn't socialize much. He was a truck driver, and she was a housewife. I started noticing that when he would come home from a run, there seemed to be a lot of traffic in and out at night, but I thought it was his friends coming to visit while he was home. The dogs would always bark, which was upsetting, but they never seemed to bark for very long.

One night the dogs barked more than usual, and I couldn't get them to stop, so I went out to check and see what was disturbing them so much. The street was lined with police cars, so I asked what was going on. They told me they were going in to raid the little house behind us as they had been dealing drugs. I told them I had noticed a lot of traffic but had never thought of that going on behind us. It was also upsetting to me because of the children.

The neighbor on the other side had a shoe repair shop about a half block from the house. He started wanting the boys to come help him. I let them go the first time, and he gave them each a quarter. I asked them what he had them do, and they said he paid them to do nothing. He wanted them to come back, and I didn't feel good about it, so I wouldn't let them go again. Then when my niece was with us, he stopped by and wanted her to go with him to check the corn but wasn't asking for the boys. I didn't let her go, and something was telling me his intentions were not good.

One of his cousins was a good friend of mine, and she would allow him to babysit her girls a lot, and he was also in charge of the youth summer activities. I got to talking to her considering his behavior. She went home and started questioning her girls to find out he had been molesting them. We reported it to the police, and they refused to do anything because he was a respected member of the community.

Because things were going well, we decided to buy a freezer and a grass-fed cow for butchering. With the things from Mom's garden and the cow purchase, we had a huge freezer full of food. In fact, there was not enough room in the freezer for all the beef; we rented a box at the locker for what wouldn't fit in the freezer.

I started not feeling well and decided to go to the doctor to see what the problem was. I told him the symptoms, and he did some tests and told me I had a sexually transmitted disease. I don't remember what it was or what he prescribed for it, but I vaguely remember him asking me if I was pregnant. I had never had a period but thought it was because my ankles were still healing. I knew I hadn't been having sex with anyone but my fiancé, so that pretty much confirmed that

41

he was being sexually involved with other women. He was always accusing me of running around on him, but we never had money for me to hire babysitters, and that definitely wasn't something you would be doing in the presence of four children.

I went for a while and still never had a period, so I went to the doctor again to find out I was pregnant with our youngest child. This was before ultrasound and all the modern technology, so we really had no idea when I had conceived. My fiancé wanted me to have an abortion and was claiming it was not his child. I stood firm that I would not take this baby's life. The doctor gave me a due date around November or December. Well, Thanksgiving came and went, and I was not even showing signs of having him. He said he would see me in a month and was pretty sure I would be having the baby before then.

The month came and went, and we still had no baby. The doctor said he would see me within the week and was sure I would be having the baby by then. We went through that for a month, and I told my fiancé that if the doctor said he would see me before the week, I was going to sock him. I went in, and he said he would see me in around twenty-four hours even though I was not having any contractions. The doctor had been after me about my weight gain, but I was down to eating lettuce and celery and was still putting on too much weight. Trust me, by this time, I wanted to have this baby.

During the pregnancy, I was always having problems with spotting. I would be on my feet trying to get things done and would then spot for two days, so I would try to sit and not do things. I wondered if I was going to even carry him to delivery. I had also felt toward the last days of the pregnancy that there was a pretty good chance I might not make it through delivery. I mentioned that to my mom, and she gave me a big lecture about creating trouble and making a scene. I told her I was at total peace about it, but I was just letting her know what I was sensing.

They were also saying there was a good possibility I would be having twins. My mother said if I had twins, she would come up and help me. I told her thanks but no thanks. We didn't get along that well. Plus, even though I loved babies, the idea of having three babies under one year of age and four under three years of age just did not sound appealing to me.

Another week went by, and on the day I was to go into the doctor, I finally started having labor pains. They admitted me into the hospital and, after a short while of monitoring, realized my blood pressure was dropping very quickly, and they needed to do something fast. They were able to get the blood pressure stabilized, and then the baby started showing signs of stress. We lived in a small community where the surgeons were flown in, and the surgeon was not scheduled to come until that afternoon. The doctor realized what was happening and said they had to do something now, or they would probably lose both of us. I gave him instructions that if it came to a choice, he was to save the baby no matter what.

They explained they were going to give me a medication to bring on the contractions harder and would then break the water at that time. They were praying the umbilical cord would not drop down and block the baby from coming. If it did, we would be in serious trouble and would probably lose us both. The doctor broke the water, and my fourth son came with the water. I had so much water that it overflowed the bucket and went into the doctor's new shoes. From what they could see, he was a healthy baby, and it was obvious he was a full term.

I was told the doctor came out of delivery whiter than the hospital sheets and apologized to my fiancé for being so hard on me about the weight. That afternoon when the surgeon arrived, I was the first into surgery for a tubal ligation. For the longest time, I had that day blocked out of my mind. I would tell people my son's birthday was February 26, and the kids would argue with me. I would tell them I should know as I was there, and I had him. I would look up his birth certificate, and they were right.

They told me, because of childbirth and having had a separate surgery, I would be in the hospital for seven days. I thought, *We'll see how that goes.* People would come in to visit and move the chairs around like so many people seem to do. When they would leave, they wouldn't put them back, so I would get out of the bed and put my room back in order. After five days, the doctor came in and said he was releasing me. He said it wasn't that I was actually well enough to go home, but they were concerned about their liability if they kept me since I kept putting furniture back in place.

My fiancé had asked his sister-in-law to come over to help with the children as I wasn't supposed to be lifting. After a week of her being there, I asked him to send her home as she and her son were just two more mouths for me to prepare for and feed. I don't think she even changed one diaper or fixed one meal during that whole time.

I had been trying to make sure the children were in church after we moved, and before the surgery, I would always take them. After the surgery, I had been told not to drive, and the children wanted to go to church. Since it was a nice day in March, they talked me into letting them walk as it was only about six blocks. I had contacted the church and told them the children were walking and if they didn't show up, to call and let me know.

Shortly after the time they showed up, one of the church people showed up at my door and said the boys had arrived, but my daughter was not with them. The story went that she was giving them a bad time, and a woman came by, asked where they were going, and said she would take her to church. They had no idea what she looked like or anything other than she was going to church also. We naturally called the police. The police chief was in the hospital but left and called in the FBI to search for her.

A couple of weeks before, there had been a young child go missing, and they had found her body the week before. I had called my mom's church, and the church was praying. The police checked the churches, and no one seemed to be aware of a little girl there who didn't belong. The second eldest, not realizing exactly what was going on and the magnitude of it all, said, "That's okay if they don't find her. You can just have another one." I did have to smile, but I also had to explain there would be no more children and that we wanted her because she meant a lot to us.

Finally, we had a breakthrough in the case. One of the churches they had checked called the police saying they had a little girl there, and no one had come to pick her up. They didn't know what to do with her. They went to the church, and sure enough, it was our daughter. The woman who had picked her up assumed they were going to the same church and took her to their church not realizing they were headed to a different one. The woman felt really bad about what happened. I could totally understand how it could happen, and I knew she had good intentions. We were just glad to have our little girl back.

There was a church at the other end of the block where we lived, and being alone with the children so much, sometimes things would get so stressful that I felt like I was going to explode. Fortunately, my eldest was really good with the kids, and I would tell him I had to get away. He always knew where he could find me if there was a problem, and fortunately, there never was. I would go down to the church, sit on the steps, and just cry my heart out. When I would get calm again, I would come back, and he would have them all happy and playing. He was such a blessing to me during that time. (He still is for that matter.)

I was realizing something was wrong with the baby. He would not stay asleep when I would lay him down. I didn't know what was going on, but I would have him totally asleep and lay him down in his crib or the playpen, and he would immediately wake up and start crying. I was being told that he just wanted to be held, but I really didn't feel that was the problem. One evening he fell asleep in his reclining infant seat, so I picked it up and took him to his bed, leaving him in it. I was concerned that he might tip it over, but he didn't; and for the first time, he slept through to his next feeding time. From then on, he slept in a reclined position in the infant seat until he outgrew it.

I was getting bad cabin fever, so I finally persuaded my fiancé to take me out for the evening. We had a young lady babysit who was the sister of a good friend of mine. He took her home and was gone for two hours even though she lived twenty minutes away. When he got home, I asked what had taken so long, and he said they had just been talking. I didn't think any more about it until, sometime later, she stopped by the house. Social services had brought her by as they were taking her to have her baby and had told her she would have to put it up for adoption. She said she had been pregnant once before, and they made her have an abortion. I never asked her who the father was or any of the details. I just remember holding her in my arms as she cried her heart out, saying how bad she wanted to keep this baby. After that, her parents would not even speak to me, and they would never let her babysit for me again. After that, she really went off the deep end and got involved with alcohol and drugs. I have seen her a few times since then, and she has gotten her life back together again, and I am thankful for that.

We found out about another house that was for sale in the community we were living in and were able to purchase it. It had been an old schoolhouse that had been brought to town and remolded. It had two bedrooms downstairs and a large family room with many large storage shelves and a laundry room.

At this point, I started wanting to get back in church. I would go for a couple of Sundays and decree to myself that I was going to live for God. Then things would get bad at home with the opposition, so I would quit going. It went that way for about a year.

Even though we had been engaged for a long time, he kept telling me he couldn't get married as he didn't know if he was divorced or not. One of his sisters let the truth out. He did adopt the boys from my first marriage, and we did get married. I realize that is all totally backward of what should be done, but as I said, I am being transparent with you. At the time we got married, I was hoping it would change things; but I really felt that if the marriage made it, it would be a real miracle. Also, during that time, my husband received a letter from a person in the military asking what his plans were concerning this woman he was engaged to in a different country. He had purchased a bar and an apartment house and left her to take care of them until he returned. I don't know what was said other than he stayed with the kids and me.

We had gone down to my mom's for the Fourth of July and were on the hill around the baseball field to watch the fireworks in my hometown. I heard a voice and was instantly paralyzed with fear. The children would ask me questions, and I would only whisper an answer. I just told them I didn't feel like talking. My husband realized something was wrong, and I told him I recognized that voice as the rapist from my first marriage. He announced he thought we would be able to see the fireworks better at a different spot and moved the car.

I thought that was the end of it. For the longest time after that, when I would go downstairs to do the laundry, clean, or put away extra groceries, I would see his bloody body at the bottom of the stairs. I would have to take authority as I could not let that vision control my life. It eventually quit showing, and I was so glad for that. Even though I had never had any training in demonic stuff, I knew this was demonic, and I could not let the past horrors dominate my life.

The baby still wasn't doing well. One afternoon I was holding him in my arms in the rocking chair, watching him fight to breathe. I was praying and asked God to either heal him or take him home to be with Him. It hurt so deeply to see him laboring so hard for each breath. I sensed God saying, *When you know what he's healed of, he will receive his complete healing.* I held strong to that for a number of years.

He would be lying listlessly in my arms, and I would take him to the doctor to be told it was an allergic reaction. They would give me some medicine and tell me to call them in the morning if he wasn't any better. I would call to find they had left on vacation. At another point, they wanted me to let them give him injections to build his immunity. I have never been one for just giving medications without knowing what they are being given for, so I decided to change doctors while also hitting every prayer meeting I knew of in the area.

One day he started coughing like he had many times before, but he didn't stop. He would cough, throw up, and start all over again. I didn't have the car that day, but we had a doctor who lived right next door to us, so I called his office. His office manager was a friend of mine, and I told her what was going on. She said she would come get me.

The doctor ordered blood tests like the other doctors had, he examined him, and his office manager took us home. She called back with the results, which said everything was normal, but added, "The doctor knows there is something wrong with your baby, so he has ordered X-rays." When my husband got home, I asked him to take us to the hospital for X-rays. The X-rays came back, and he didn't have an inch of air space in either lung. It turned out he had a viral pneumonia. They immediately hospitalized him.

He was in the hospital for three weeks, and none of the medications they gave him were working. The doctor finally told me, "We have one last medication we can try, but it will probably cause his permanent teeth to come in black." I told him I didn't care; I just wanted my baby well. I walked out of the hospital room that night, and I really had doubts that he would make it through the night. The next morning, I walked into the room to be met with a huge smile, and I knew things had finally turned. The doctor did admit that whatever the problem was, it was beyond what he was able to handle, so he referred me to a specialist in a community about an hour away.

During those three weeks while he was in the hospital, I had gotten the older boys sent to school, a friend came to stay with the second youngest, and I went to the hospital to be with the baby. I got a call from the school that they needed to send the second eldest son home as he was sick. I don't remember how he got home, but I do remember my daughter was with a friend of mine in the mountains. It turned out the son they sent home had the chicken pox. My friend's husband had never had chicken pox, but she said she would stay and help for a while. She was such a blessing. I really don't know how I would have made it without her.

A couple of days after the second eldest was sent home from school, the second youngest also developed chicken pox. The second eldest was just returning to school when the eldest came down with them. In the meantime, my friend who lived in the mountains brought my daughter home, and she came down with them. I was so tired, especially after my other friend was no longer helping with the children. I had always thought my mother's phrase of being bone tired was such a stupid comment. I got to experience it, and it was not fun.

We lived about two blocks from the hospital, and when my friend was no longer at the house, I would feed everyone at home breakfast; send the one who was well to school; walk to the hospital to feed the baby and get him back to sleep; go home to try to get some work done and lunch fixed for the ones at home, leaving the older ones to keep an eye on the younger ones; go to the hospital to feed the baby and get him down again; go home to fix dinner for the ones at home; go back to the hospital to feed the baby and get him down again; and walk back home and fix dinner for my family. I was so tired that it hurt to take the next step, and to add to it all, the ground was covered with snow.

I asked my husband if he could please help me some by coming home earlier than his usual nine, which was five hours after he got off work. He informed me that if I was taking better care of myself, maybe he would have a desire to come home. My hair was never done. At that time, it was almost waist length, and I would wear it in a ponytail as I really didn't have time to mess with it much. I went in and cut my hair an inch in length all over my head. My hair had enough curl; I always called it African bush, so by cutting it, it actually laid nicer, but it didn't resolve the problem as he still wasn't coming home until the time he had been before.

At the time, I was also selling Artex paint tubes and was being very successful with it. We had a convention in Omaha, and we had planned to go. Since the baby was doing well, we arranged for Mom to go with us to watch the kids while we were at the meetings. The baby started coughing again, and I knew I had to get him to the hospital. I had lived with this long enough that I just knew when I had to take action and never even realized how frightening it was to someone who had never experienced it. Mom had never been around when he would have these attacks. She told me later he was so blue that she didn't think we were going to make it to the hospital in time.

Even though we didn't know Omaha, we were able to find an emergency hospital; and after they examined him, they sent us directly to Creighton University Hospital. They got him stabilized, and the nurse told me to go home and that she would make sure he was well cared for. That was the first time he had ever seen a black person, and he was afraid of her. I tried to comfort him, and he wouldn't be comforted. I did leave as she said, and the next morning, a couple of hours later, I came back, She was sitting there, rocking him and singing to him. From then on, he was fine with black people.

His roommate was a little boy with sickle cell anemia, and no one ever came to see him. I asked the nurse, and what she said just broke my heart. She said that, many times, when the families would receive that diagnosis of sickle cell anemia for their child, they would walk out of the child's life and never see them again. The little boy was so sweet.

After four days in the hospital, they released my son to come home. The family had already headed back without us as they needed to get back. The doctor's last words to me were "You get him out of here within the next twenty-four hours, or he will be back in the hospital." I caught the first bus out of town, and before I left Omaha, he was starting to cough again.

We had to cancel his appointment with the specialist as we weren't going to make it home in time. The specialist realized there was a serious problem and set aside a new time. When we got home, I took the baby in to see him. We talked about what had happened, and he said, "His problem is beyond my expertise." He started making arrangements to get him with an asthma allergy specialist in Denver.

Things got really crazy from that time on with all the specialists and testing. The office worked really hard to get us into the one specialist as quickly as possible. We went to the appointment and, after they examined him, informed me he had asthma and asked if any doctor had checked his ears. I didn't remember them being checked, but by that time, I had been through so much with him that I didn't notice a lot of things. Both eardrums were on the verge of bursting.

He immediately called his top ear, nose, and throat specialist, who said if I would come right over, he would stay open late to evaluate him. We got over there and, after the examination, were informed both eardrums were on the verge of breaking from the infection, and he needed drain tubes in both ears. The asthma specialist had prescribed a nebulizer with treatments every two hours around the clock and respiratory therapy every two hours. Between the times required for the treatments and the nebulizer, it would take thirty minutes. They informed me if the asthma was not cleared up, they would not be able to put the drain tubes in, and it was vitally important that the pressure be released from his eardrums so as not to cause problems with his hearing.

I don't remember how many days I was given, but when it came time for the surgery to put the drain tubes in, he was no better. We discussed the options, and since he was a mild-mannered baby, we decided that we would try to not totally put him under the anesthesia. He did do fine, and later, we had to put drain tubes in a second time.

The doctors at National Jewish were able to get him under a grant to find out all his problems. I was very thankful for that as they had five specialists for him. I would get to the hospital, and the specialists would meet me at the entrance and take the baby from me. From then on, I felt like a dog trying to follow after my master. They would play with him and totally keep him entertained while asking me all kinds of questions. I would leave feeling like a wet noodle because I was so drained, but we were finally getting some answers. They decided to start giving him his vaccinations and had a full staff alert until they knew he was out of danger. His whole body did swell up from them, but it didn't affect any of his vital organs. After all the testing they found he had been born with an immunity problem and Chronic Asthma. His immunity count was only fifty where a normal CBC is 500. That explained why the blood tests always came back that he was not sick.

I came home on the bus after he had received one of his shots, and there was a couple on the bus who worked with my husband. They asked me where he was that I was trying to take the bus with all his equipment and a baby that was so sore. I told him what my husband had told me, that they wouldn't let him off. The man said he was the one to whom those requests were submitted, and he had never received a request for time off.

Because of what we had found out about the baby, I was told if he started showing any signs of getting sick, I needed to get him to the doctor immediately. We had so many emergency calls, and our new doctor was working very closely with the specialists, which made it so much nicer. The new doctor told me one day to just call him when the baby was showing signs of distress, and he would meet me at the clinic even if it was on a weekend to save on emergency costs. He would leave family dinners to meet us so we could do everything we could to keep him from going back into the hospital.

I had been offered a state position with Artex, and I really struggled with it. It would require a lot of travel, but I thought that if I was able to get a really good position, maybe my family would finally be proud of me. I wanted so badly to be accepted by the family, but I knew I had to do what was right for the children, so I declined the position. I finally resolved in my mind that even if I became president of the United States, it still wouldn't change how they thought of me, and my children were worth far more than that state position. It wasn't too long afterward that Artex sold out to our competitor, and I refused to switch because the competitor had an inferior product, which I would not sell to my customers.

I realized during this time that I had stockpiled household supplies and canned goods so that we were able to live for three months from what I had on the shelves and in the freezer. Since we were getting low on beef, I had gone to get some of the beef out of the locker box to discover that someone had taken half of what was there. All that was left were the less desirable cuts like the neck bones and such. My husband and I talked it over and decided we weren't paying for the box any longer, but we didn't have room in the freezer yet for the rest of what was there.

Later, we received a letter stating that there were new owners, and they wanted us to pay the bill. We talked it over, and my husband said not to pay it, but there was something inside of me that kept feeling like I should. After all, it wasn't the new owners who had stolen the meat, and they shouldn't have to suffer for what the previous owners had done. Finally, I felt so strongly about it that I went and paid the bill. I told them what had happened and explained I didn't feel they should have to sacrifice for what the others had done and that I prayed they did well. By then, with all the hospitalizations and trips to specialists, the freezer was close to being empty.

A couple of weeks later, I received a call from them, and my first thought was *Why would they be calling since the bill was paid?* When I called back, they said we were the only ones who had paid, and they wanted us to have the meat from all the locker boxes that hadn't paid. They did say they didn't know how good it was as some had been in there for quite a while, but if we wanted it, we were welcome to have it. Some of it was freezer burned, but I would cut the burned part off and cook it with some spices and was thankful for the meat to feed my family. We were buying milk from the farm as the store-bought milk would give the baby diarrhea; it was a real blessing as they were selling it to us much cheaper than we were paying in the store.

One of the times while I was in Denver, taking the baby to specialists, I called home to see how things were going. My husband informed me he had just bought a house in the town where he worked. We had talked about purchasing a house there since gas prices were getting so high, but he hadn't even discussed this with me. I asked him how much he had paid for it. He informed me had had gotten it at a sheriff's sale for $23,000. That sounded okay, but the next questions really troubled me. I asked where the house was, and he said he didn't know. I asked how many bedrooms it had, and he said he didn't know. All he would say was that it was a really good deal.

I fretted and stewed the whole time I was in Denver. I couldn't comprehend buying a house that you had no information on. It was about three months before I knew where the house was or the size, and that was after they moved the people who were in it out because they wouldn't pay rent or try to buy back the property. They had put it in the hands of a litigator or something like that to see if they would give us rent or work with us before they evicted them.

The day the people were moved out into the street, I got this call asking if I was proud of myself for moving them out in the street like that and their little boy coming home from school to find all his stuff out in the street. I asked the person what she was talking about because I had no idea what was going on. She told me they had moved the former owner out in the street. I told her getting possession of that house was the least of my worries at that point as I had the second youngest in the hospital, and they were saying it was kidney problems. The doctor had diagnosed it, and the specialist said the doctor didn't know what he was talking about as he didn't see a problem. Later, we found the family doctor had been right.

She did apologize, but it was through her I found out the address of the place we had bought. I had sold Artex to the owner and always had a problem getting my money. I had drunk coffee there and at least had an idea of what the kitchen was like. When I was able to go in, I cringed to think I had drunk coffee there as the cabinet shelves were so sticky and grimy that it almost made me sick to look at them. It was a huge house on a corner lot with a two-car garage. The house needed a lot of work, but it definitely met our need for the family. It had five bedrooms, a bath and a ¾ bath, a huge kitchen, a breakfast nook, a living room, a dining room, a utility room, an office, a playroom, and a partial basement.

By now, I had pretty much decided I would divorce my husband, take the big house, and let him have the small house in the community we were living in. I was tired of men having all the rights and being irresponsible, so I was going to join the gay lifestyle. I was tired of being treated like a doormat and like a piece of property.

Chapter 7

The day we were to start moving, I knew we wouldn't be able to start as my husband worked the bar the night before. I decided we were going to turn over a new leaf in our life. I got the kids up early, and we headed to our new community to go to church.

We got there early, and the couple I sat next to was from the community we were living in. It was starting to snow, and I mentioned to them what a day to decide to move. They offered to help us as they had a van, and we could get it done faster. I can't say I remember what the pastor spoke about that morning, but he gave an altar call, and I and the couple headed to the altar. We all gave our hearts to the Lord that day. I was also filled with the baptism that day with the evidence of speaking in the heavenly language. We grabbed some lunch and then started to load their van and our vehicles to start the move. We actually became very good friends, which lasted until they left the area.

The house needed a new roof before the loan company would give us the loan. I mentioned it to some of the church people the following Sunday, and a number of them said they would help us the following week if we had the shingles. I told them I would talk to my husband and let them know. He said that would be fine, so we set up the time, and they all came over. With all the ones who came over, we had the shingles replaced within a short time. There was still other work that needed to be done, but it was things that could wait.

After accepting Christ, I realized I needed to give God a chance to see if He could make a difference in our marriage. Between the people I had met at church and the friend who helped me when the children had chicken pox, we were moved in a short time, and the friend helped me get things cleaned and put away.

I loved the house and the church. Because of all I was dealing with, it was like I was walking around in this cloud, and I have to admit there are a lot of things I don't remember that well.

On July 3, 1979, just three months after becoming a Christian, I received a telephone call saying they wanted my brother and me at Swedish Hospital in

Denver the next morning about something concerning Dad. I don't even remember how I received the message as I was at a church picnic when the message came in. I immediately started making plans to be there. We had no idea what to expect as Dad was healthy and had even, just a few days before, loaded a large vending machine in his van by himself. It seems to me like my brother picked me up, and we had ridden together.

We met with the doctors to be informed he had acute leukemia, and they figured at most he had six months to live. To complicate the issue, they had perforated his esophagus in trying to find out where the bleeding was coming from. He had gotten into a lot of natural health remedies and many times had told us about how people had seen miracles by this method. He had always been such a fighter, and with his natural health diet, we decided to tell him, thinking he would fight and beat it. He seemed totally content to just accept it. The doctor had said, because of his age, they didn't recommend chemotherapy or radiology. He was less than a month of being seventy-nine years old.

After Dad and Mom divorced, because the church had been so harsh toward him, he had gotten involved with a religion that believed in reincarnation, and so had my brother. Since we had time before the meeting with the doctor, my brother and I decided to visit Dad's church. Even though they were singing songs like "How Great Thou Art," something just didn't seem right to me, so I started praying quietly in the spirit. The pastor got up to speak, and he was really having trouble giving his message. When the service was over, my brother commented he had never heard him have that much trouble ministering and that it was like he had his tongue wrapped around his eyeteeth. I knew it was God and that what I had been sensing was spiritual warfare.

The man who I remembered was a student of the Word of God (my dad) did not even want us to read the scripture to him. This really concerned me, and I had expressed it to Mom. My brother and I stayed at my dad's apartment, and his girlfriend joined us for a while. There was one time we got lost trying to get back to my dad's apartment, and we were in the black part of Denver, which at that time was a high-crime area, especially for white people. I actually felt safer there than I did with the people/spirits I was keeping company with.

A friend had told me that one time, when she had to have surgery, she was concerned about leaving herself open to evil spirits, so she asked God to protect her subconscious mind. God reminded me of that, so before I would go to sleep at night, I would ask for God's protection over my mind as I slept. I woke up calling the name of Jesus, and his girlfriend, who was sleeping beside me, was thrashing around. I knew God was answering my prayer for protection of my mind as I slept.

He seemed to be getting better, and a chance opened up for me to go home. The baby had had an asthma attack but not serious enough to need hospitalization, which was a relief. The warfare had been so intense, and I had not been able to go anywhere without someone accompanying me. As soon as I got home, I didn't even stop to go get the children; I immediately went to the pastor's home and talked to him about what I was up against. Then I went to get the children and was glad to be back with them.

The next afternoon, I received a call that my dad had taken a turn for the worse, and I needed to get back to Denver. I called Mom and told her so she could tell my dad's sister who lived in the same town. I was getting ready to head back to Denver when Mom called back saying for me to meet my aunt at the airport in my hometown as her son was flying both of us to Denver. It was such a relief to not have to make that four-hour drive. My mom's sister picked us up at the airport and took us to her house.

My brother said he didn't want us talking with Dad without him there, so he was supposed to pick us up the following morning to go to the hospital. We waited and waited, and my brother didn't show up. Finally, my mom's sister said she would take us. She dropped us off at the hospital, and my aunt and I stood in the hall and prayed for God to open the door so we could talk to Dad about his need to know he was ready to meet God. As we were praying, a nurse walked by and asked if everything was okay. We explained we knew he didn't have much longer to live and our concern about his being ready to meet God. She said she would be praying with us. I knew the church was also interceding on our behalf. We then went back into the room to be with Dad.

God is so cool. He let a total stranger do it for us. The daughter of Dad's roommate came into the room and was talking about how wonderful her church service had been. She looked at me and said, "I understand you believe in reincarnation."

I replied, "Not me."

Dad piped up that he did. She started by saying that Dad could come back to this earth as a skunk if he wanted to believe that way, but when she died, she was going to go to heaven to be with Jesus. She would be walking those streets of gold with her heavenly Father and having a wonderful time. She must have gone on for about a half hour while my aunt and I sat there, trying not to smile, just holding each other's hands, knowing God had intervened in the situation in a way that only He could. When she finished, my brother showed up. I don't remember why he had been late, but I realize it was a God appointment.

Since my dad started doing better, my brother decided to go home so he could go to work. My aunt went home, and the next day, another one of my Dad's sisters came. We visited, and then she left. Later that evening, my stepbrother came and took me out to eat. Everything was pretty much closed as something had happened, and the hospital was operating on auxiliary power, and they were limiting water. We did find a place to get something and went back to the hospital.

The next morning when I arrived at the hospital, Dad was up and coming back from the bathroom. He took hold of his wrist, raised his arm, and let go of it, and it dropped down beside him. He said, "See this?"

I said, "Yes, I saw you raise your arm up and let it drop."

"I can't raise it without using my other hand." He admitted he had gotten up to go to the bathroom unassisted and had fallen. The side that was giving him problems was opposite of the side he had fallen and hit his head on. I just assumed it had been from the fall, but now I wonder if he had suffered a stroke. They had him on morphine to alleviate the pain.

As the day went on, he continued to go downhill. Toward evening, they had given him a shot of morphine, and he was begging for something to help with the pain less than fifteen minutes after the shot. I knew things were getting bad. I tried to adjust him and told him they couldn't give him anything more for the pain until that had a chance to wear off, or they would be overdosing him. When I finished adjusting him, I told him there was really nothing more that could be done humanly, but God had promised if we called on His name, He would answer.

> Adonai is close to all who call on him, to all who sincerely call on him. (Psalm 145:18, CJB)
>
> And then, whoever calls on the name of Adonai will be saved. (Acts 2:21, CJB)
>
> Since everyone who calls on the name of Adonai will be delivered. (Romans 10:13, CJB)

I continued to stand by his bed and hold his hand. I heard him say "Jesus, Jesus, Jesus," and he lost consciousness. I asked God to give me confirmation that I would see him in heaven.

I felt God saying to me, *At six o'clock sharp, he will see the new dawning.* I called the family and told them he had lost consciousness and that I thought they needed to return.

The doctor came in for the blood transfusion they were giving him every four hours. There was a shortage of blood in the city, and Dad had a really rare blood type. I asked the doctor what would happen if we discontinued the blood transfusions. He said, "I wouldn't be seeing you in the morning." I told him to discontinue them as we knew Dad wasn't going to get any better and maybe that blood could save someone else's life.

My brother and his wife showed up at around ten o'clock. We could feel a breeze, but there were no windows open, nor was the air conditioner running. My husband finally showed up at around two in the morning, saying he had gotten lost and then had trouble getting into the hospital. Dad's temperature had risen to 108 degrees, and the gurgling from the damage done to his esophagus was getting worse. A nurse walked by his room and came in to check him. He let out his last breath, and she announced it was six o'clock. The breeze stopped at the very minute he breathed his last breath. We all discussed it and felt that the breeze was angels waiting to take him home. I knew God had given me the confirmation that he was in heaven.

We had the funeral that weekend. My stepbrother was a florist, and we had almost as many floral bouquets as we did people. The floral arrangements were huge and gorgeous. It was almost like they were trying to outdo one another, and there were flowers I had never seen before.

I stayed in Denver for the weekend as I had a doctor appointment on Monday with another specialist. The baby had started bleeding internally. We were trying to find out what was causing it other than reactions to some of the medications they had him on. I explained to the doctor what we had just been through, and he started apologizing as they had to redo a test to see if the baby had intestinal cancer. You could tell he really felt badly, and he also said he could understand my fear as he had lost his son to intestinal cancer. They did find eventually that the problem was polyps in his bowels, and they said if they broke off, he could bleed to death before I could get him back to Denver, and Denver hospitals were the closest with equipment to do that kind of procedure on such a small child.

I got home after losing my father, and all these people who had been continuously calling and spending hours on the phone with me were no longer available. I hadn't liked talking with them on the phone that long, but now I would call them, and they didn't want to even talk with me. I asked God what was going on. He told me they didn't know how to deal with death as they had never lost anyone. Their way of dealing with it was not dealing with it. The pastor and his wife were there, but they were the only ones. It really hurt, but God was faithful and saw me through it all.

A couple of months later, a friend's husband called me in the middle of the night saying she wanted him to call me as something strange was going on. He put her on the phone, and the minute she started talking, I picked up on a demonic spirit trying to possess her. I was never trained in any of this, but I knew instantly what was going on and what I needed to do. I prayed over her, commanding the spirit to leave, and she calmed down and gave the phone back to her husband. We hung up, but I still didn't feel a release, so I went to the piano and started playing and praying until I felt a release to go back to bed. I had also called my pastor, and later, I found he had been praying into the middle of the night also because he wasn't getting a release.

Because of what I had experienced with my father and what I had experienced through her, I asked my pastor, "Is this the direction God is taking me for my future?"

He said, "I think it is just coincidental. It probably won't happen again." Well, it didn't for a while.

I saw a documentary on TV about what they called the "bridge people" in the town where the rapist from many years ago had lived. I was so burdened for those people and the bondage they were in. I felt God was telling me that I needed to go minister to them about Jesus. Being married to a nonbeliever, I knew it would take a miracle for me to be able to go. Finally, I told God I would go if He wanted me to even though the cost might also mean the sacrifice of my life. As soon as I said yes, the burden lifted. I asked God what was going on, and I felt like He was saying, *I just wanted to know if you were willing.* I found that lesson very valuable over the years. Sometimes we feel He is calling us to something, but all He may be asking is if we are willing to go. Always make sure to wait for His confirmation and direction.

We were starting a building project as the church was getting too small for the congregation. I took every opportunity I could to help with the building. Sometimes I would help with meals, and sometimes they would actually trust me with a hammer. It was exciting to see the people working together to see the building completed. The morning we were able to move into the new building, we all met at the old church, and the ones who were able walked together to the new sanctuary.

I was able to go to a women's conference in a neighboring town and was excited to finally get to go to a few things. The speaker talked about doing things for the Lord. If you have ever been in a small church, you know that, many times, they will ask people to do things, and the person will do it as they see there is a need, and the space needs to be filled. That day, the speaker asked us how many things we were doing in the church. I proudly counted the many things I was doing. I was doing fourteen things. I have to admit I was so proud and felt like I was really doing a lot for the Lord. Her next question really burst my bubble. "How many of the things you're doing has God called you to do?" I went home and, after praying and seeking God, resigned from ten things. I was so busy doing what I thought I was supposed to be doing for the Lord that I was neglecting some very important things I was responsible for. I have to admit that in my entire Christian walk, I have had to be careful to keep that in balance as I love doing things for the Lord.

Shortly after that, they asked me to work as a volunteer in the office doing the bulletins and things. It wasn't a lot of hours, but I loved what I was doing. They did eventually start paying me $50 per month for the work I was doing. Also, it wasn't very long afterward that the pastor resigned, saying he felt God was calling him to start a new church in a different area.

In the pastor's parting message, he spoke on how Samuel went to select the first king of Israel and thought Saul's eldest brother was to be the king. God told him not to look at the person but to look at the heart. When they started the selection for pastor, there were a couple of people in the church who had decided whom they wanted. He had a lot of good qualifications, but he was not voted in. The selection committee called some others to come and try out. One was really good and said he would come, but there had to be a unanimous vote, or he wouldn't come. There were two who dissented, and they were the ones wanting this other pastor. The ones who had dissented for that pastor to come wanted the one they wanted to come again. I don't remember if he refused or if he came and set criteria that wasn't met. Anyway, he didn't come.

Then they received an application from a pastor in a very liberal state. He came and tried out and was voted in. Before he came, one of the board members' wives called the office and expressed concern about the pastor even though she hadn't met him. I told her we just needed to pray and trust God. He was voted in. Later, I heard another board member's wife comment that it was time we had a handsome really young pastor. She felt he would be a real asset to the church. My spirit cringed. I hadn't felt he was to come but knew we had to accept what had been decided and pray.

He moved with his family, and one of the first things I heard from his family was that God had called him to our state but not them. It wasn't too long until I could see some real problems starting to evolve. One intercessor asked me how things were going, and I replied to her that I felt like I was an office manager to a harem. I think it kind of shocked her, but she did inquire for more information. Women were coming to the office to counsel with him with their blouses unbuttoned past their cleavage; they were coming to change clothes, polish their nails, and all kinds of things like that. He was always flirting with them and encouraging them on. In the summer, his wife and children would go back to where they came from for the summer. One time I stopped at their apartment, and I had someone with me. He answered the door in his underwear. I don't know if that was a common thing in his former state, but it wasn't in our area. I found out later I wasn't the only one he had done it to.

Before I quit and moved, I was afraid to send the board members down to the basement if they came to talk with him as I didn't know if they would find him with his clothes on or find him running around in the nude. His excuse was that it wasn't wrong to admire God's artwork in the beauty of the body. After I was divorced, there were a couple of times he demanded I remove my clothes; and I hate to admit it, but I obeyed. He never touched me though.

The second youngest son was still having problems, and they couldn't find out what it was. The doctor said he thought it was ulcers. I disagreed with him as he would get sick from eating rice as quickly as he would from eating chorizo. There was never any consistency to his getting sick. He would start throwing up with no warning, and after he threw up, he was fine again.

One day a friend of mine had taken cupcakes to the class to celebrate her daughter's birthday, and I had received a call to come get him as he was sick again. After school was out, she called me to tease me about how her cooking was not really good, but it wasn't so bad that my son should turn green and throw up. I commented, "He didn't really turn green, did he?"

She said, "I kid you not. He turned green and threw up."

I thanked her and called the doctor. He ordered a test run on his kidneys.

They said it would only take two hours, but three hours later, they came out saying they had stopped the test as the die had not even made it through the kidneys yet because there was an obstruction. The collection area would have to be totally rebuilt, and there was some kidney damage. It basically confirmed what the previous family doctor had said, but the specialist disagreed with him.

I cried to the associate pastor, questioning why he hadn't received his healing. Of course, in some situations, we really have no answers on this side of heaven. The associate pastor said he had no answers but was reminded of an old song, "I Don't Need to Understand, I Just Need to Hold His Hand." I did find the song, and it has helped me so much over the years with the things I have gone through and also in counseling people going through rough times.

This child was also asthmatic, making that surgery a high risk of him getting pneumonia. We were told he would be one week being turned manually and to plan on at least five weeks of hospitalization. I was beside myself with fear. I had asked many to pray and believed for his complete healing, but God had different plans. He went through the six-hour surgery, but he was only in the hospital for five days. Pneumonia did try to set in, but they kept on top of it, and it cleared out very quickly. The hospital staff was amazed at how well he did. After five days they did release him with catheter care, but they trained us in what to do so we could care for him at home.

In the course of that year, we not only went through his surgery but the baby continued being in and out of the hospital and having testing, the second eldest had an emergency appendectomy, and my husband broke his leg playing baseball as well. The day I received the hospital bill for the kidney surgery, we also received a bill from the state of Oklahoma for the same amount, saying it was for back child support on my husband's children from a previous marriage. I was totally overwhelmed with it all and also angry as he had told the courts when he adopted the boys that he had been paying support to his other children. He said it was supposed to have been taken out of his military retirement and he would get it taken care of.

The emergency appendectomy had to be done in a neighboring town as there were no surgeons close, and for them to fly in with the anesthesiologist would take better than an hour, and we didn't have that kind of time. My neighbor said she would ride with me, and she had a gas card; back then, you had to have a special card to pump gas after hours. We checked him out of the hospital at 11:15 p.m., filled the tank, and had him completely checked into the hospital by midnight. The trip was normally an hour drive. I was told later it was against the law to transport a patient with an IV without medical staff, but no one had told me. I had my flashers on, hoping I would get stopped; but evidently, there were no policemen on that section of road that night. I would look in the rearview mirror, and there was a string of cars following me until I turned to go to the hospital, and then they turned off.

After surgery, they said it had been burst for a while as it had a sac that had grown around it. He did end up with a longer stay as his temp was elevated because of all the poison from the burst appendix in his system. I praise God for taking care of him as many people have died from a burst appendix, and we had taken him to the doctor a number of times about it and was told it wasn't that serious.

We were finally getting a good report on the baby. We had taken him to Denver again for more blood testing. The letter we received back said his progress was miraculous. His immunity count had started to increase, and if it continued to increase at that level, they would release him from their care. He was scheduled for more tests in six months. Those tests also came back with miraculous improvement. Even though they still weren't at the level they needed to be, the doctors felt it was okay to release him from their care at that time. That was his first testimony in his Sunday school class, that he no longer had to go to Denver and get all those needles put in him for the blood tests.

The eldest boy was giving problems at school, and the school suggested I take him to a psychologist. After examining him, they told me I needed to get him into a private school as he was bored with school. The school system had been dumbed down so everyone could make it, and they weren't moving fast enough to keep him interested. He never did his homework but could pass his tests and was always disturbing the class. I knew we had to do something quick so he would not flunk his classes. There was a private school close to my mother, but it was an hour away from me. I really wanted to keep him at home if at all possible.

I had been praying for God's guidance on what to do when the new pastor, who had been there for about a year, and the board decided to put in a Christian school. They decided this in May and planned to be open in the fall. They had decided to go with a curriculum through the Baptist Church called Accelerated Christian Education (ACE). We started taking applications and testing the students to see where we needed to place them so we could order the necessary curriculum to start school. We started out with thirty-six students. They had decided to have me start working full time and were giving me $250 per month. I loved working at the school and the new challenges it had for me.

It was a real challenge for me to get all the information received from the schools charted and filed along with all the information concerning the applications and tests organized for the start of school, but God was faithful, and I was able to have it completed by the time we opened school. We started after Labor Day and had most of the supplies needed to start. I had worked many nights until almost midnight to have my part ready to go before we opened, but I felt fulfilled on opening day. There were some things we didn't have in place at start-up like PE, but God brought volunteers along who were willing to help us fill in the gaps.

Someone had donated an Apple IIe to us with no instructions, disks, or manuals, so they decided to send me to a class to help with it. We had bought a printer, but because we didn't have the program disk, it wasn't really user friendly.

I did finally figure out how to get it so I could use it similar to a typewriter and was very pleased about that accomplishment. It turned out that the class was just learning the computer terminology. The instructor would tell me to execute the program, and I would put in commands to get it to run, and they never seemed to work. I would find myself thinking, *If you would give me a gun, I will gladly execute this program.* I did finally complete the class and passed it, but it really hadn't done me much good to work with what we had to work with. Finally, someone told us they needed to purchase a floppy disk with the program on it to get it to work well for us. After that was purchased, it was a lot easier.

I enjoyed working with the children and getting to know all of them in the school. Sometimes some would come in, and it was obvious their day had started out badly. I would catch them as they came in and would get permission to take them out to talk. We would get in the car and drive around until they had talked it out and were ready to go back to school. Many times, I would go out with them during my lunch and play football with them even though I was in a dress and high heels.

One came and talked with me about wanting to see revival fall on the school and our area. For quite a while, he and I would meet in the sanctuary and pray during lunchtime for revival. A couple of others joined us for a while but eventually fell away. After a while, he quit coming in also. I went on for a while but eventually stopped.

One day I had this knock on the door. I opened it to have one of my husband's ex-sisters-in-law at the door. She announced to me that she had heard we had bought a different house, and she was coming to see what her new house looked like and wanted a tour. I was furious and thought how brazen to do something like that. Every time I would try to talk to him about problems I felt we were having, he was always threatening to divorce me instead of trying to work or talk them out. I had gotten to the point I was so tired of his not wanting to resolve the problems and the women, I would think and finally got so I would say it: "Don't let the door hit you in the butt on your way out." And here, she announced she was moving in with him after I was out of the picture.

Sometime during all this, I found out just exactly what my husband's nephew had done to my son. The reason I said "son" was that the other son had never admitted it, but I do suspect he was also molested at the same time. I received a call from my mom, and she was very upset, telling me what she had discovered. I don't remember if all the children were down with her or if there were just a couple of them there with her.

Because of the nature, the county sheriff had been notified. We lived in different counties, so there were two counties involved. The local county sheriff called and talked with me about it. He asked if I wanted him to tell my husband as he had worked with him and knew how hard he could be. Usually, I would deal with things myself, but I asked him if he would tell him. I called work the next morning and told them I would not be in to work because of a family situation. I fell on my knees before God for guidance to know what to do and how to walk through this.

My husband was blaming me, the church, and the Christian school but would not accept that it was his nephew. I was told because of what had happened, I was going to have to bring charges against my son. Since it was a small town, I didn't feel I could really talk with anyone as I wanted my son to be able to come home when this was over and be able to start over. I also knew I had to get him the help he needed. I did tell the pastor and the school director. And as in most of the things in my life, they didn't know how to deal with it, so I was pretty much left to walk through it alone.

The day they took him away, I took him in my arms and told him, "You may hate me the rest of your life for what I have to do, but I know I have to get you the help you need. I will always love you no matter what." I stood on the street alone, crying, as they took my son away in the sheriff's car to take him to a boy's home in a community about two hours away.

I was only able to go see him once during the six months he was there. At that church service, the pastor was ministering; and even though I don't remember a lot of what he spoke on, I remember the testimony of Dave Reeves that he shared. Dave was in the military in Vietnam, planting acid bombs along the river. Snipers shot at him, hitting the bomb he was planting, and it went off. He went under once, twice; and the third time before he went under, he threw his arm in the air and shouted, "My God, I still believe in you!" God gave me a musical narrative from that testimony, and later, I was able to meet Dave and share with him how inspirational his testimony had been to me during such a time of deep heartache. The boy's home was good in a lot of ways as my son was able to experience a couple who honored and respected each other. I do thank God for that.

During this time, I started asking God to put someone in my life whom I could trust and who would not judge or gossip and would be lifting me in prayer. One day one of the older ladies in the church came to mind, and she had invited me to come visit her on the farm some time before. I called to see if I could come out to just get away from things. While I was there, she asked me what had happened, and I was able to share with her. It was such a relief to finally have someone to share with about the things that were happening.

When my son was allowed to return home, we were told there had to be some changes. He had always been my enforcer, and they would no longer let him help me in making the kids obey. We had some major adjustments to make. I had always appreciated having his help, but now I was totally on my own.

Also, during this time, I started coughing up blood. I said something to my husband about it, and his response was "Yeah, run up a bunch of doctor bills so I can't divorce you." I was so hurt and didn't know exactly what to do. I sought God and felt He was telling me to research into natural vitamins to turn the situation around. I said something to my mom, and she sent me some money to purchase them. For quite a while, I took a handful of vitamins as the instructions said each day. The situation finally turned around, and I was no longer coughing up blood. Somebody told me I was probably suffering from stress asthma, but I don't know for sure.

Thanks to some who were willing to give scholarships, I was able to put all five children in the school. During the summer months when the children weren't in school, I would walk to work in the morning, walk home at noon, walk back, and then walk home in the evening. It was good exercise for me, but it also allowed some emotional healing. I would actually march, and all the way, I would be saying, "I am a king's daughter. I have value." I was trying to get my mind changed from what I had always been told.

I was still suffering from suicidal depression. One day I went into the sanctuary and told God I was not leaving until He revealed to me why I was having the depression and why it was always the worst around Thanksgiving and Christmas. He revealed to me that the suicidal depression came from transference of spirits when I received the clothes from my aunt who had passed away in a mental institution because of being suicidal. He also told me that I was angry toward Him for taking my favorite aunt. I argued with Him for a while and then finally decided I would ask Mom when the aunt had passed away. She said it was somewhere between Thanksgiving and Christmas. That confirmed it, so I asked God to forgive me for being angry with Him and allow my favorite aunt to go home to be with him. I wish I could say I was instantly healed, but I had many years of "stinkin' thinkin'" to reverse before I would be completely whole.

I was also able to find out more about the death of my aunt whom my grandmother said I reminded her of. It was during the depression years, and my mom worked at the courthouse. My aunt was a kind of free spirit, and the reason I say that was that the only picture I saw of her was the last one taken, which they had inserted in a family picture. She had earrings on, and that was something most people didn't wear during that time and definitely not teens. She was sixteen when she passed away. There had been a prescription at the pharmacy for my aunt, and my mom was also to pick up a prescription of cyanide to kill the mice at the courthouse where she worked. My mom picked up the prescriptions, and within twenty-four hours, my aunt was dead. They said the labels had been switched, and my aunt had taken the cyanide for the rats. I am positive my mother was not responsible for the switched labels.

One day as I was talking with someone about it, God told me that was why Mom never wanted to develop a relationship with me. Every time she would look at me, she was reminded of that day and felt guilty. It was never investigated as my grandparents didn't have the funds to hire a lawyer.

Some new people started coming, and I really hit it off with one woman. Her mother-in-law was also an intercessor and had also moved to the community.

We actually got to know each other at a parade that was happening in town. As the friendship developed, God was taking both of us into some things we had never walked in before, but we were willing to follow God's direction, and the mother-in-law was very supportive. We felt like we were supposed to go around the community and pray. She had broken her foot, so we agreed to do it after she got her foot out of the cast.

Two days after her foot was out of the cast, on a Saturday morning, we started our walk. It took us four hours to walk around the circumference of the community. We would pray over things we felt God was telling us to and in the way He directed us. We prayed over the places of government, but we also prayed over this one person's house. I felt led to pray against anorexia. I had no idea if the resident was suffering from that even though I knew them. I knew she was way too thin but didn't know if that was the problem. Another prayer was for this man who kept driving by and looking at us. We felt he had a drinking problem and prayed against it.

When we finished the prayer walk, we did ask God to reveal to us that we had heard Him about the things we had prayed about. The next morning, the man showed up at the house, wanting to talk with one of the boys. He obviously had plenty to drink, and it was before church that he showed up. The one whom we prayed about anorexia started putting on weight and looking a lot healthier. What was also exciting was that my friend's foot did not hurt at all. We knew that was God.

It was with her that God started me into spiritually cleansing homes. I had opened up my home to a young mother at the request of her grandmother. I don't know what was going on, but for some reason, she was leaving her husband. I remember the room she was in, but I don't remember how I had arranged things so she could stay with us.

One night she came home, and I was in the bath after doing my usual weekend cleaning. She asked if she could sleep in the playroom as it was so hot upstairs. I told her that it would be all right and didn't think any more about it. I came out of the bathroom, and the knife drawer was open. I thought that was kind of strange as that was something I never did. I shut the drawer and headed to bed.

One of my sons came home and asked if she had come home. I told him she had asked to sleep in the playroom, and I asked why. They said she had met up with a man that night who bragged about killing his best friend, and she had planned to go meet him. I told him to go look, and she was not in the playroom or in the house anywhere. She had climbed out the back bathroom window and went to meet the guy. That made me search the knife drawer a little better, and my favorite knife was gone. I never did find it, so I don't know what happened to it.

I immediately called the grandmother to let her know what was going on. When they did find her, I would not let her continue to stay, but I had felt there were some demonic things that had happened in that room. My new friend agreed to come and pray with me for it to be cleansed.

Neither of us had done anything like this, but we sought God on how to do it and made plans to meet to cleanse the house. We started out by having the kids go to a friend's place. We prayed for ourselves and protection over ourselves and our families. After we felt God was giving us a release to start, we started upstairs. The first two rooms were fairly easy. When we got to the room she had been in, the door slammed shut and locked. We tried to unlock it and couldn't do it. We prayed over the door for a while and then went outside and prayed toward the room. We did this a couple of times before we were finally able to unlock the door and cleanse the room.

We finished cleansing the house, and the kids came home. They all commented on how clean the house smelled. We knew we had dealt with demons that night as we cleansed the house.

There was a woman who came regularly from the nursing home. I had helped with nursing home services on Sunday for a number of years, and most of the people talked about how this woman was so hard to deal with. She didn't like TV and didn't want many other worldly things in her room. Finally, they had given her a private room as no one could get along with her. I found myself judging her, but when I got to know her, I could understand. She didn't want anything to interfere with her spending time with God.

On this one Sunday when she was at church, we had planned on singing her favorite song "Just A Closer Walk With Thee" and dedicating it to her as she was going to the hospital for her second amputation. The musicians continued playing during the interlude, and we all had tears in our eyes by the time the interlude was over. She had continued singing, and there was an angelic choir singing with her. It was so beautiful, and when the service was over, we were all asking one another if they had heard it.

My neighbor across the street and I had never met, but I knew her husband from my bartending days. He was the mortician and came in quite a bit. One day her boys were over, playing with my boys, when my dog bit her son. I was sick as we always tried to keep him on a chain as we knew he was very protective of everyone and everything. This day, the kids had let him loose in the yard, and they were all playing with him. The one boy loved dogs and leaned down to give Teddy, our husky, a hug. Teddy bit him and put a huge gash along his jawline. Of course, he went running home, and the children came in and told me what had happened.

I kept trying to get in contact with her to find out how bad it was, and it was taking forever. Finally, she got home with her son. He had nine stitches along his jawline. We had a nice talk, and she said she had instructed the boys not to come over if the dog was loose in the yard. They said as long as the dog's shots were up to date, they were not going to file charges or anything since her son had disobeyed. She and I became the best of friends and would walk in the mornings together and have coffee before going to work. Only God can bring about a good friendship from a dog biting someone's son.

When the woman for whom we had sung "Just a Closer Walk with Thee" died, since we had not used any of the snow days up for the school that year, we decided to call a snow day for her funeral. To have the funeral dinner, we would need to dismantle the school in the basement, and the funeral dinner would interfere with the school classroom. The day of her funeral, we got up, and it was snowing. It snowed so hard that we just about couldn't make it to the church for the funeral, and it was two days before they could get her to the cemetery. The next day, the neighbor came over for our usual coffee, and she said her husband wanted to know how we could call a snow day when the weatherman had even missed the forecast. I just smiled at her and told her to tell him we had a direct line. She laughed, saying, "You must have."

The school decided to have a field day, and we took the students to the organ grinder. At that time, it was a famous pizza place with an antique theater organ. It was housed in six buildings around the main building. Many times, I didn't get to go on the field days, but I was excited to be included in this one. The organ had five keyboards and was huge. They asked if I would like to play it, and I jumped at the opportunity. It didn't take much to make the furniture vibrate. At first, the size of it was intimidating to me; but eventually, I got to the point I was enjoying myself playing on it. It was one of the highlights of my life.

A certain person had done a number of things that had caused problems for my family, job, and home. One time I went into church early on a Wednesday night to be jumped about something she had said. I left the service and drove for a while and then cried out to God as I felt so alone. Jesus reminded me He understood how I felt as when He hung on the cross, His own father turned His back on Him. Another time, God told me that what she was telling was to get people to look at me and get their eyes off her as she was the one doing what I was being accused of. Later, that was also confirmed. It still didn't make it any easier, and I knew I had to forgive her.

One good thing about that pastor was he did get me to start to open up about my past. The first time I talked about it, I started crying, and the cries were coming from my innermost being. It felt like my insides were going to come out as the sobs were so hard. He also told me that when things were so bad that I didn't feel like I could forgive the person, I should ask God to help me forgive them until I could walk in total forgiveness. That was a very valuable lesson for me to have learned over time.

One day I was sitting at the desk at work and heard a voice saying, "Call a lawyer." The school had gone on a field day, so there was no one there. I thought that maybe someone had slipped in without me noticing, so I looked around to see if someone was there. I didn't see anyone, so I went back to work. Like Samuel, I heard the voice again saying the same thing. I looked around again and still couldn't find anyone. I went back to work and heard the voice a third time, only this time it said, "Call the lawyer now." I realized it was God speaking to me. I know God speaks against divorce in the Bible, but He also talks about knowing a person's heart.

I picked up the phone book, found a lawyer, and called. That particular lawyer wanted to take my husband to the cleaners. That wasn't what I wanted. I didn't want to be vindictive in the divorce; I just wanted out of the abuse. I found another lawyer and called him. He consented to take the case, and I drove to the neighboring town and retained him for the divorce. I can't say it was what I wanted, but I had talked to my husband about us getting counseling to try to work things out, and he always refused.

I had gone to a neighboring town to get some counseling and also contacted some pastors who basically didn't know me as I wanted to make sure I had plenty of counsel from experts and people who were knowledgeable in the Word. The counselor got after me, saying I was trying to blame myself for the problems. I told her I was trying to be totally honest with her as she could not help me unless she had the total truth. When we finished, she said it looked like he wanted a divorce, but he wanted me to look like the bad one. I walked down the street and looked in a shop window, and I was standing tall and proud, which I didn't remember ever doing. Both pastors said it was not God's desire for a woman to endure abuse or adultery just to make the marriage work.

I had also gone to our family doctor during the difficult times. He gave me a choice of taking a two-week vacation away from everyone or admitting myself to the hospital. I knew we couldn't afford for me to take a vacation, and I also knew the hell I would go through if I did. As a result, I went to the hospital. The kids followed me in, and it looked like they were in a funeral procession. I had sung in a group with the doctor, and he was surprised at what I was going through. My mother was taking the children for the time I was in the hospital.

It got so bad in the hospital that the nurses wanted me to get a restraining order or let them refuse to let him in. I told them I had to face it sometime, and the hospital was the best place. His mother and sister showed up; they seldom ever came. His sister whom I had been close to at one time picked up on what was happening and mentioned something about it to me. I just confirmed it to her but didn't go into detail.

One of the things my husband had me upset about was he said he was on the verge of losing his job and that it was my fault. I couldn't understand why as I never called or went to the office unless there was an emergency. Finally, I called his supervisor as I had known him from my bartending days. When I told him what I had been accused of, he informed me he was not on the verge of losing his job; and if he was, it was not on account of me as I was never around. If he was on the verge of losing his job, it was because he was so hard to work with, and they had problems getting people working with him.

It didn't help that someone supposedly in the know told him I was having an affair with the pastor. It really hurt as I had tried to have such discretion that even if we were working on something together, I would not go on his side of the desk, and I always made sure the door was open. During that time, he wouldn't even speak to me for three months. When I asked what the problem was, all I would get out of him was that I knew. I tried telling him that if I knew, I wouldn't have asked. Before that happened, he was starting to come to church with us and wasn't spending as much time at the bar. My children were finally getting to experience a normal life and no longer had to walk on pins and needles when he was home. After that, he would no longer go to church with us, and he went back to his drinking. It was really hard for me, and I struggled with anger and bitterness toward the person who had caused such devastation to our family. I was finally able, with God's help, to forgive her for what she did.

Chapter 8

We got a call one day asking for my husband. The person on the other end was saying he was my husband's youngest son from his first marriage. I was so thrilled that God was answering my prayer for him to be reunited with his family. I have to say I had very mixed emotions as I had wanted so badly to meet his children, but I also knew that the marriage was over, and I didn't think I would be able to develop a relationship with them.

His son said they were coming to visit in July. I was excited as they did come and stay at the house while they were there. I was blessed with the privilege of getting acquainted with him and his wife and getting to know them for the first time. They commented how much I reminded them of his mother, which was a surprise to me. They also confirmed that I was very wise in not letting our daughter be with him alone. We did develop a good relationship over the years before my husband's youngest son passed away.

Nobody had told me when the papers were being filed for the divorce., I came home one night and it was obvious he had been there, but I didn't know what was going on as it was rare for him to be home that early, and it was obvious he had left. Later, I found out they had served him the papers; and the chief of police, concerned about my safety, took him to the house and told him to get the things he needed.

From the time I had filed for the divorce, I would come home from work, get the kids to bed, and go out walking around the community, crying and praying for God to spare me from having to walk through this. I know God was protecting me as I would be out walking in four-inch stilettos and a dress for hours. It was during the winter, and many times, there would be ice on the streets. Sometimes my feet would be so cold that I couldn't feel them, but I would continue to walk and pray. I do thank God that no one stopped and talked to me. I really believe He hid me as I was walking so I would have that private time.

At one time, my husband said he wanted to work things out, and I told him I was willing, but he had to get rid of the other woman. He informed me it was my fault that she was in his life and he was holding on to the relationship. I told him then I wouldn't even talk to him about reconciliation as long as there was another woman in the picture.

We did go to court right after he was served to at least set temporary arrangements concerning the divorce. He was to take one credit card, and I was to take the other one. They decided on temporary child support until the day of court and custody of the children.

He had never gone to any of the children's activities, but suddenly, he started showing up at their ball games. When the game would be over, I would look for them and not be able to find them. When I did find them, I would find they were with him. He said the children were supposed to let me know they were going with him. I told him it was his responsibility to make sure I knew they were going with him. He was not to be taking them without my knowledge. I talked to the lawyer about it, and they put a restraining order against him, by which he did not abide. I could have pushed it but didn't want to cause problems; I just wanted something that was workable between the two of us.

On what would have been our anniversary, I received a bouquet of flowers at work. Everybody thought it was so wonderful, but I was pretty skeptical as he had never given me flowers or done anything for our anniversary. I commented that, with the way he was doing things, there was a good possibility it had been put on the credit card that I was responsible for. Sure enough, when the bill came in, they had been charged to my card.

That year at Christmas, still hoping we could possibly work things out, I invited him and another friend of the kids to Christmas dinner. In the middle of dinner, my daughter yelled, "Daddy, stop that!" I asked what he was doing, and she said he was running his hand up and down her leg. I told him to stop, and he replied that she wanted it. I blew up. I told him just because she wanted to be close to her father did not mean that she wanted him to be doing those things. I knew then I had to go through with the divorce, and I thanked God He had protected me from going through something similar to that again.

The day finally came for the divorce. I can't say I was looking forward to dealing with my husband, but I was looking forward to having this all behind. We got to court, and I was in for such a big surprise. My husband said he wanted both houses. At first, he wanted it so the children and I were just put out in the street with no place to go. I fought to at least have one house. Then he decided we could live in the big house and make the payments on it, but when the last child left home, I was to get out, and it would be his. My lawyer wouldn't even fight for me. He was willing to let my husband have whatever he wanted. I fought for the big house. There was a second mortgage on it, so we finally came to the agreement that the big house was to be mine. I was to pay the first mortgage, and he was to pay the second. The big house needed some repairs, and he was to make the repairs. The little house was in good condition, and it would be his.

The credit cards were going to stay the way it was decided in the temporary arrangement. We decided on the amount of child support which was one-third of what our annual income was a year. He said he was not going to pay the child support at all. He was to maintain the insurance as it was provided through his work. He refused to take visitation rights, and finally, it was decided that he needed to let me know twenty-four hours in advance if he wanted to spend time with the children, and he was to pay the attorney fees.

Fortunately, the place he worked had a policy that if their employees didn't pay their bills, they would be fired. Because of that policy, I did get the child support because, at his age, he was getting to the point it was not easy to find another job.

About six months after the divorce, I ran into an old friend, and she asked how I was doing. I told her I was doing fine and that everything was good. She looked at me again and asked, "How are you really doing?" I burst into tears. I told her I had thought, once the divorce was over, things would get better; but here I was, crying every time I turned around. She told me about the grieving process. She had lost both her boys in a very tragic accident and had done an in-depth study on grieving. She took the time to tell me that even though it wasn't a human death, there had still been a death of a relationship. She told me that I was just going through the grieving process and to give myself time, and everything would be good again.

After we talked, we realized I was getting a double whammy as I had never grieved over the first divorce. I had been hit with so much after my first husband walked out on the boys and me, and it threw me into survival mode. I thank God for running into her and being able to learn about it. It has also helped me with counseling other women who are walking through the same process.

I had tried to sell the house as I knew we really needed to get out of the area. I just wanted to walk away from all the heartache and move on. I started talking to people about possibly selling the house. Everyone I spoke with who was interested would change their mind when they found out they would have to deal with my husband on the second mortgage. They all said they didn't want to even work with him. I wasn't sure about what to do as I knew I couldn't make the payments on the house and also rent something else. I was trying to weigh all my options.

The eldest went into the army after graduation, and I went out to see his graduation from basic training. There had been a man whom I had been seeing after the divorce. I came home to find he was seeing other women, and I ended that. I knew it wasn't a healthy relationship as I had gotten involved with him sexually. I wanted so much to be loved since I hadn't been held by anyone in years except for my husband, who only held me when he had sex with me which was not often at that point. I had let this man use my car as his vehicle had broken down, and he needed transportation for his business since he was a tree trimmer. Later, after I sold it to a friend, I found he had cracked the head on it.

That fall, we came home one night from school/work, and the electricity started doing some strange things. I called the city electric services to see if they could find the problem. They came and checked the meter and the pole and said everything was fine there. They said it had to be in the house, and they weren't supposed to do any work in a house, but because of the situation, they would go in and check things if I gave them permission. I gave them permission, and they found out that the ground wire had been disconnected. They put it back and told me that had we not caught it, it would have caused all the appliances to burn out and could have caused a fire. They also said that it had to have been done by someone who knew our schedule and was familiar with the dogs.

It was reported to the police, and they were pretty sure who it was but couldn't prove it. They said they would be watching the house closely. A couple of weeks later, we had the same problem. I called the city again, and they came out to check things. This time, the problem was at the pole. I realized then that for the safety of the children, I had to move.

I did quit my job at the school, and the doctor I had sung with offered me a temporary job setting up their new filing system. I was enjoying meeting new people and having a different work environment. One day I received a bill from them, and I didn't know why as the children hadn't been in. I asked the office staff what was going on, and they looked to see what they could find. It turned out my ex-husband had been in for a physical, and he told them to put what the insurance didn't cover on my bill. The gals in the office were furious when they found out what had happened and did take it off my bill. They said when they confronted him about it, at first, he said it wasn't his. They showed him it was his bill, and he did pay it.

As much as I hated doing it, it was decided that I would move back with my mom. That Christmas, my brother and his wife came, and we moved back to my hometown. Later, I could see that God had His hand in it, but I do have to say I was really struggling with it at the time.

I was able to find a job working at night taking care of an elderly lady, and Mom would be with the children during the night. I was homeschooling one during the day. The eldest was in the military now, so I homeschooled the second eldest as we didn't feel it would be good for him to have to transition from private school to public school during his last semester. The youngest, they decided, would be best put into special classes for half the day and regular classes for the other half because of his health issues until he could get up to the scholastic level he needed to be. The other two were going to the public school full time.

I discovered there were problems developing. The children would tell me one thing, and Mom would tell me something different. I realized this was a repeat of the problem that I had with Mom and Grandma. I decided I needed to do something, so I started looking for a place to live. I was finally able to find one on the east side of town. The price was right, but it did need a lot of cleaning. It did make it a little bit harder as there wasn't anyone there for the children when they arrived home. They were old enough to be home alone, so that wasn't a problem; I just liked to have them supervised.

I started working at the hospital part time in the X-ray department, did some home health care, and also started doing some transcription. I do admit the transcription was hard as it was a totally different language, and I hadn't typed for a while.

My second eldest decided to stay with my mom since he didn't want to share a room with the two younger boys. He was preparing to go to the navy upon graduation anyway, so I couldn't uproot him once again. He wanted to get a car, and I kept telling him it wasn't wise as it would be sitting while he was in basic training, and he would be on ship six months out of the year, at which time it would also be sitting somewhere. My ex-husband was supportive of him getting it, so he did. I still don't remember how my name ended up on the loan, but it did. He was supposed to have an allotment set up for payment to be made out of each check to cover his car payment.

I had been convinced by one of the government departments for helping single mothers that if I went to college, it would make it easier for me to get a job. There were some good plans available that could help me with the expenses. I applied for the programs through social services. It was something I had always wanted to do, so I thought it was great. My first classes were through Regis University without Walls. I waited for the funds to come in, and they didn't come. I would contact the student loans department, and they would say the college had them and that they had been credited to my account. The school would not let me start classes until they had their money. I kept getting a runaround and wasn't getting anywhere. Finally, I got angry with them; and suddenly, the funds were found. There was another woman registered whose name was Elizabeth Jacobs except she had a different middle initial. They had given her my money. Once we were able to get that straightened out, I was finally able to start my classes.

I had to start making payments on my son's car, but I wasn't getting any of the money for those payments. He kept telling me he had it set up and that they were taking it out of his check. I kept calling, trying to get to some solutions, and wasn't getting any answers. I was getting really upset with my ex-husband as he was a retired military and could have helped with the problem since he would have known the right departments to contact. Because of all the calling concerning his loan and the student loans, I ended up with the phone disconnected as I could not make all those payments on the child support I was getting and my pay.

I finally was able to get the money to get the phone reconnected but not without all kinds of problems. I sent them the money they needed to get the phone reconnected. I waited a week and still did not have a phone. I used my mother's phone and called to see what was going on. They never did receive the check. I checked the bank, and it hadn't been processed. I called them, and I specifically told them I was sending another check and that I had put a stop payment on the other one. They confirmed there would be no problem if the other one arrived; they would not cash it. They got the second check, and I was thrilled to have my phone back.

I came home from work that night to not have a phone. I called them to see what was going on. They said they had received one check, put it in the bank, and reconnected the phone. Then they received the second check, and the bank wouldn't process it, so they disconnected my phone. I tried explaining what had happened, and they could see the bills had been paid but proceeded to tell me that to get the phone reconnected, I would have to pay another reconnection fee. I flat let them know that I wasn't paying a second reconnection fee when it was their incompetence that had caused the phone to be disconnected. I shouldn't have to pay for their mistakes.

My mother and one of my sons were listening to the call. Mom thought I should become a consumer's advocate, but I told her no as I didn't like the stress. My son was saying, "Mom, that was so cool. You can put those big companies down so low you can step on them when they try to mess with you."

They finally got things straightened out with the grants and loans so I could start my college classes. I was so excited, and the first week of classes went really well. The Friday assignment was to make a schedule for the following week as it is important for you to schedule your day. I had tried that before, and it never seemed to work other than for the routine things I did like work, church, and meals. I had my schedule and thought I was ready to go.

That Monday, I got the children off to school and was getting ready to leave for work when I received a call from my daughter saying she had forgotten her school book and really needed it. Usually, if they forgot something, I would not run to get it for them; but for some reason, that day, I did. I got to the school to realize there was an officer behind me, and he turned his lights on. He came over and asked me if I realized I was speeding. It is a problem I have always had, but I honestly had no idea how fast I was going as all I was thinking about was getting the book to her and getting to work. He only cited me for a seat belt violation, which I was thankful for, and it was one, I will admit, where I was walking in rebellion about having to wear one. I headed to work and finished my job of cleaning the woman's house and headed home to finish preparing for classes that night.

I arrived home to find a note taped to my door from my mom's former pastor. They were heading to her place to take her to the hospital. I immediately hopped back in the car and headed to her place. They had her almost out to the car, so we put her in my car, and I headed to the hospital. I got her registered and stayed with her until it was time for class. So much for that schedule as the rest of the week when I wasn't working, I was at the hospital. I had known she was very sick when I took her but hadn't realized how sick until she had been in the hospital for three days. She looked at me and said, "Beth, I think you need to get me to the doctor as I'm very sick." I told her she was in the hospital already.

My eldest brother and his wife came down to help me not only take care of things at her house—she had lots of potted flowers—but also with decisions. They kept running tests but couldn't find anything. Finally, they decided they wanted us to take her to the closest large hospital with a resident radiologist as the radiologist wouldn't be in the local hospital until the following Wednesday. They were at least able to narrow down where the problem was. My brother brought her back with no diagnosis.

That early Sunday morning, I received a call from my brother; the hospital had called. All her vital signs had gone crazy in the night, and they were going in for emergency surgery. They discovered that about a foot of her intestine had died, and that was the reason for the problem. (When she got well, she blamed it on the apple juice she had been drinking and refused to drink apple juice again.) She had a do-not-resuscitate order in place, but the physicians doing the surgery had known her all their lives, and even though she expired on the operating table, they wouldn't let her go. The reason I know is that I was still working at the hospital part time, the surgical nurse and I were friends, and she let it slip.

Mom did have a lung collapse during the surgery. They released her to go home, and a niece was going to stay and take care of her, with me going out every so many hours to give her respiratory treatments. Because of the baby's problems, I was well trained in the treatments and I give credit to God for preparing the way for her care. We were praying for the lung to inflate, and one day when I went out, she said she had a really bad coughing spell. The lung had inflated, and we praised God for that.

I found she was really clinging to the walker. I knew that with the way she was walking with it, she was very apt to have it roll out from her, and she would fall on her face. One day she needed to go for an evaluation, so I put her in the car and took the walker back to the house. My niece was asking what I was doing, and I just flat said she didn't need it anymore. I wasn't going to let her become dependent on it. We got to the doctor's office, and she complained to him about it. He looked at my mom and said "Well, good for her." From then on, she continued to graduate until she became completely independent again.

My daughter started having problems with her tonsils, and the doctor was saying she needed them out. I had submitted the papers for the medications to the insurance agency with payment to be made to me for reimbursement. I never received the money. I told my ex-husband she needed to get them out, and he said the insurance agency required a second opinion. I took the day off from work and took her to a different doctor for a second opinion. Later, I received a call from the insurance administrator asking why I took her to another doctor. I told her my ex-husband had told me I needed to. She said, "We have a Cadillac plan, and there is no need for a second opinion." I realized once again I had been had. I never did receive the insurance payments for her medicine. Later I found he had changed the forms so the payment would go to him.

We got her tonsils out, and when the bill came in, once again, I filled the paperwork out to go to the provider. They billed me again. When I called the provider, they said they had never received payment. I called the administrator, and she said it had been paid, but it had been set up to be paid to my ex-husband. By then, I had had enough. I asked her if she would be willing to go to court with me about it. She said yes, but she would talk to him. She called back saying he had received a payment from the insurance company but didn't know what it was for, so he pocketed it. I knew he had to have changed who it was to be paid to as I had put it to go to the doctor, and they wouldn't have changed it on their own. Within a couple of days, that bill was paid.

My son was to graduate from the navy, and I was really feeling I was to go but didn't want to leave my daughter, with her being in the hospital. Some friends from church who had connected with the kids said they would take her while I was gone. I talked it over with her, and she said she felt like I needed to go also, so I left her with them and headed to his graduation. My pastor was originally from that area, and his former church consented to provide a room for me at a hotel there. I prepared some food to put in the ice chest so I wouldn't have to stop at the restaurant on the way and started out.

I had $10 in my pocket and a gas credit card. I was driving my son's car as it did get better gas mileage. When it started getting low, I pulled into a truck stop to see where there might be a filling station I could use my credit card at. They said there wasn't one for a long distance. I debated what to do. Finally, I decided I would put $5 in the tank and go as far as it would take me, hoping to find a filling station that would take my gas card before then. I got back on the highway to find the filling station I needed at the next exit. The whole trip was a walk of trust in God. From then on, every time I would get low on gas, the right station would be at the next outlet, and I would fill up.

At one point, I did get tired, so I pulled over in a rest stop, rested for an hour, and headed back down the road. I got to the city where the naval base was and pulled in to get gas and ask for directions to the hotel. The cashier was so rude to me and refused to help me. I was so tired that I almost broke into tears. I made up my mind that he was not going to intimidate me, and he wasn't going to see me cry. I bought a map and tried to figure out which way I needed to go. I knew what street was next, and if it wasn't, I needed to turn around and go the other direction. I also knew I had to be careful not to get on the toll road as they charged at every toll gate. The pastor had warned me of that. Well, I started the wrong direction and had to turn around; but I did find my way to the hotel, got registered, and got my things in the room.

I headed to the base just in time to catch the last bus to the ceremony. After the ceremony, I went back to the hotel and was looking forward to a refreshing shower and some relaxation. I had just finished my shower when I heard all this commotion in the hallway. My first thoughts were *Oh no, someone's having a party and there is going to be all kinds of noise.*

Then I heard someone yelling, "Fire! Fire!"

I grabbed my Bible and headed for the lobby. I got to the lobby, and my first thoughts were *This is nice. I am to go to a naval graduation tomorrow morning, and I get to go in my housecoat with my Bible.* It turned out to be a false alarm, so I headed up to read some from my Bible and go to bed. I got to the room to discover I hadn't grabbed the keys to the room, and I was locked out. Inside, I was laughing at myself and all the humor in all of it. I headed back and apologized to them for the inconvenience, but I had locked myself out of the room. They laughed with me and let me in the room. I did call to see how my daughter was doing, using the last of the money I had.

The next morning, I went to the graduation and was able to spend some time with my son. The morning after the graduation, I headed back home, and he headed to his next assignment of duty.

The return trip was pretty much uneventful, and I was glad for the quiet and the time to be with God. I love to drive as it gives me lots of God time. The one thing that did happen was there was a caravan of trucks that kept passing me and slowing down. I thought it was a little strange and had decided I would not pass them again. The one in front pulled out to go around me and started crowding me off the road. I had the car on cruise control, and as I realized what was going on, my first thought was *This car doesn't have enough power to power out of this spot.* I was almost off the pavement when, suddenly, the car just shot ahead. I still did not have my foot on the gas pedal, and I realized God had gotten me out of the situation. I remembered the scripture that said, "He will give his angels charge over me." And I had once again experienced it in a supernatural way. I continued on to the next truck stop and waited until they passed the exit before pulling back onto the highway.

With trouble finding full-time work, the problems with the educational funding, the problems with the money to pay for my son's car payments, and the problems the children were giving me, I decided it wasn't worth the fight. One of the children had started getting abusive, and when I called my ex-husband to ask him to take them as I couldn't take it anymore, he said, "No, I won't take them, but I will talk to them." One of them told me all he had said was that I was under a lot of stress and to be more understanding toward me.

One night I decided to end it all and took a large bottle of ibuprofen. I had thought of all kinds of ways to do it, but I didn't want it to be really traumatic on the children. I woke up the next morning as though nothing had happened, and I was so mad at God for letting me live. I had gotten the children off to school, went into the bathroom, and cried. About that time, my mother came in, not even knocking on the door, and informed me she had come to put the shelves together she had given me. She said, "I see you have already put them together." And she waited for me to come out of the bathroom. I didn't come out until after she had left as I didn't want to face her; plus, I was upset about her coming into my house without even knocking. It wasn't until a long time later that I even admitted to anyone what I had done.

My coffeepot was starting to act like it was about to give out on me. I was so excited that I found a coupon where I could get a coffee maker for free, no shipping charges, if I submitted the lid from four coffee cans with the brand name on them. The coffee brand was what I always used, and I always saved the cans to store extra sugar and things in. The morning the new coffee pot came in, my daughter had asked me for money for something, and I told her I didn't have any. She came home and found I had this brand-new coffeepot sitting on the counter. She was so mad, saying I had lied to her, but then had gone out and bought this brand-new coffeepot for myself. I explained the coffee maker didn't cost me a thing. I have never seen a coupon like that before or since. I knew it was God providing a coffee maker for me at the time I needed it. Once again, God was confirming that He takes care of His children. The old coffee pot quit that very morning which also shows God's perfect timing.

I realized that the University without Walls was really not my forte. I found I wasn't having any socialization and was becoming way off balance. My life consisted in work, church, the kids, school, and studying. As a result, since most of my classes through the university were also through a local junior college, I decided I would just sign up for campus classes. I usually drove my son's car as it had better gas mileage, and it was working well.

One day as I was heading home, a woman hit me. I am thankful I was taking business law as the class had prepared me for some of the things I was going to have to deal with. I saw her coming from the south and realized she wasn't even going to slow down for the intersection. I hit the brakes and skid the length of the car when she hit me. The accident happened about a half block from the police station, so I made sure she was all right and ran to the police station. They came out and took pictures, filing a report.

I called my insurance agent, and he said he would take care of it and told me some of the things I needed to do. After I had taken it in for estimates, their adjuster called me and told me what he was going to offer. He said they would only pay for so much because of contributory negligence and that I was traveling too fast for approaching an intersection. I knew what he was talking about. I talked to my insurance agent, and he informed me I would have to accept his offer. I informed him I wasn't taking it as the accident had not been my fault.

I went to the police station and asked to look at the pictures. I wasn't even in the lane of traffic. The pictures showed a car parked about halfway down the block, and I wasn't even out past the middle of that car. My insurance agent said if

I didn't accept their offer, I would have to fight it myself. I did, and I won. I should have also gone for a front-end alignment, but I didn't think about it at the time.

The next semester, my daughter had an accident, totaling her brother's car. When she called telling me she had an accident, she had walked to the nearest farmhouse, and I told her to stay put and to call the police. I was backing out of the driveway to go to the accident when the younger boys showed up with some other friends who were like brothers to them. They knew something was wrong, and I took just long enough to tell them there had been an accident. Their comment was "Don't have an accident going to her accident." They knew I had a tendency to drive fast. I was able to get there before the officers did. I picked her up and went to where the car was. I knew the minute I saw it that it was totaled. After the police investigated it and released us to go, I really sensed I needed to take my daughter in for X-rays as she was saying her back hurt some.

We pulled into the hospital, and many of her friends were waiting for us as they had heard it on the scanners. They took the X-rays, and because I had worked in the X-ray department, I asked to look at them. The doctor said her back looked normal, but I disagreed and told him, "These two vertebrae don't look right." I want to say it was L4 and L7, but I don't remember for sure. He said she was fine and to send her to school the next day.

When the radiologist came in that Wednesday, I was on the phone asking if he had read those X-rays yet. He said he hadn't, but since they were my daughter's, he would read them first. It wasn't very long when I had a call from him wanting to know where she was. I told him they had told me to send her to school. He was very upset and told me to get her home as she had one splintered vertebrae and one that was broken. I realized once again how faithful God had been as she could have been paralyzed or severely damaged her spine with walking the distance she had after the accident and not having the proper care.

I went to one of my classes after that, was telling the young lady sitting next to me about her accident, and commented that I sure hoped the claim wasn't going to be the hassle mine had been last semester. She asked me about the previous accident, so I told her about it. Then she asked if that happened around Christmas and if I always called toward evening. I responded, "Yes, it was." She said her father was an adjuster for the insurance company I had battled with. She said the person who would call made him so mad that he would slam down the phone from talking with them and cuss. She said no one had ever beaten him or won when they contested his adjustments. Once again, I knew God had given me favor.

I was going to be able to graduate from Northeastern Junior College that spring with the requirement of taking a couple of classes in the summer to complete the requirements. I knew if I continued with them, it would be night classes from then on, or I could transfer to a different college and complete my bachelor's. To complete my bachelor's at a different college would require moving. I had looked at a couple of out-of-state colleges, but the children didn't want to go out of state, and they were saying their father would fight me if I tried to do it. I don't know if he had really said that or if they were just saying it. The children wanted to move to a big city and had selected one they thought they wanted to live in. I applied to the university in that community and was accepted. I was so pleased to have a 3.87 GPA as a nontraditional student, pulling 18–21 credits a semester, driving three hours a day twice a week, and working part time.

I had managed to find a job at a reservoir for the summer working in the store. Overall, I loved working there, but it meant I had to work on Sundays, and I really missed church. The owner was really great to work for, but the coworker was something else. One day he told me he would pay me $25 if I would come early and do work for him. He also said I could make more prostituting than I was getting paid. One day a child came in with pennies to purchase something, and he threw them on the floor at the child. I knelt down, picked up the pennies, and counted them so the child would have his stuff paid for. I talked to the owner, and he said he couldn't let the coworker go as he needed him for doing repairs for the docks and boats. I told him I understood and that I would be quitting early for that reason. We both understood the other's situation, and I did run into him many years later, and he was still apologizing.

I had suspected my daughter was pregnant, but she had told me she wasn't. It was during this time when I was looking for a place for all of us to live that she confirmed it. It was really hard as I felt like I had finally gotten to the point I could see the light at the end of the tunnel of raising children and was hit with the responsibility of another child. I had many people telling me I should kick her out or make her have an abortion. I stood my ground that I wasn't going to make her have an abortion, and I was not putting her out on the street. She was just a child herself, and I was going to try my best to be there for her. I also felt that, because of her age, she needed to make the decision on what she was going to do as she would have to live with it for the rest of her life. I was doing a lot of praying and was so thankful that she decided to carry the baby to term. She wasn't sure if she was going to allow the baby to be adopted or not, but I was going to take one step at a time. While going to the city to find housing, I found a beautiful card and wrote a note to her, telling her how proud I was of her for making the decision she had made.

While I was making those trips back and forth, I would go and stay at my eldest brother's after I got off work and then the next morning drive over to look for housing and then head back home. One morning I came out of his bathroom with a smile on my face. He asked what happened in the bathroom that made me so happy. I had always considered myself an ugly duckling as I never felt like I fit in anywhere. I had looked in the mirror that morning and felt like God was telling me I wasn't an ugly duckling but a beautiful swan. I told him about my experience, and he said he had known that all along. (He used to refer to me as a bulldog as if I grabbed hold of something I wasn't going to let go, but that was when I was younger, and all my pictures at that age had that look.)

Chapter 9

I found housing just a little better than a week before I was to start classes. It was a very small apartment, but we were able to make it work. We joked that the kids could change channels on the TV from the couch without ever having to move. The week we were to move, the second youngest had his tonsils out. My eldest was out of the service and living with my mother with his fiancée and her son, so they were able to help with the move. We loaded the cars up the night before, and then I stayed with my son until he was out of surgery. We left for our new home in the city, unloaded the cars, and returned home so I could be with my son and get ready to take another load.

We got settled in the house; I got the kids in school and had found a job by the time my classes started. I found that I had already taken three of the classes the adviser had put me in, and they were limited drop classes. I had three days to get out of them and get a class to replace them. I kept trying and trying, but since they had a new enrollment system, it wasn't equipped to handle the load. I was told they were closed down at night. Well, I decided since I had to get them replaced, I would go in really early in the morning and see if I could get it done. At three o'clock on the last day, I was able to get them changed. This put me three days behind on those classes, so I had to play catch-up.

I was excited, thinking things were finally going to calm down a little. Then Desert Storm started. My second eldest son was on ship, waiting to go to the Mediterranean. My eldest son had received word he was being reactivated. While his fiancée was packing to move down with my mom since he had gotten a job in the capital city by then. The little one got into a box his fiancé had already packed, drank gun cleaning fluid, and ended up in the hospital. My mother started having ministrokes and thought I should come home to take care of her. With both boys in the military now and headed to areas of conflict, I had to admit I was spending all my spare time in front of the TV, trying to keep informed with what was happening with my boys. The boys' biological father called and asked me how I was handling it. I wanted to reach through the phone and strangle him. I was so angry. How did he think I would be handling it? My son's fiancée was able to get moved down to my mom's, and I kept trying to keep on top of things there.

My eldest brother did step in on the situation with Mom and said I was not to be moving back. I needed to start doing what was best for the children and me. That helped relieve some of the pressure.

I ended that semester with a 2.0 GPA. Everyone who knew what I had been dealing with was amazed that I came out that well. I had to give all the glory to God, and I was excited that I hadn't failed any of my classes.

Having come from a small town where you never locked your doors, it was hard for us to make the adjustment of always locking the doors. One night I heard the door open, and my first thought was the kids were coming home from the recreation center on the property. I laid there in the bed when, suddenly, this figure of a man showed up in front of my bedroom door. He was so tall; he had to duck his head to enter the room. I threw back my covers and yelled, "What are you doing here?" He closed the bedroom door, and I heard the apartment door close. The person wasn't staggering, and with how quick he got out of the apartment, I knew he couldn't have been drunk. It took me a while before I could go lock the door, but from then on, the door was always locked by the last person through at night. I don't know what his intentions had been, but I know God had once again protected us.

The next semester went a little better. We had been accepted for government housing, so we had planned to move. The place we were in had come furnished, so now we had the problem of needing furniture. We had realized Mom could no longer take care of herself. We had tried hiring a caregiver and found that not only was she getting paid but she also was stealing the professional permanent wave solutions from Mom's beauty shop and selling them. We knew that wasn't a liability we wanted to take, so we had to fire her and make a decision on what to do with Mom. My eldest brother decided he would take her to live with him for as long as they were able to do it, so I was blessed with the furniture. Once again, I was able to experience God's perfect timing. We were able to get settled before the baby was born.

My beautiful granddaughter was born, and she was such a joy, but I do have to admit there was a certain part of me that resented the extra responsibility. We had tried to get help with her, and once again, I was hit with the choice of putting her out so she could get help or us trying to make it without the help. We didn't know what we were going to do for day care either. I had called and called the Department of Human Services, and they would never return my calls. Finally, I remembered that one of our former neighbors before I was divorced had said her son worked for the Department of Human Services. I didn't know if he still worked there or not, but it was worth a try. I called his parents and was informed he did still work for them, and his mother gave me his direct line. We were making progress. We were at least able to get her on a program and got the day care set up. I know it was just God who opened up those doors.

I had talked to the college about the following year, and they said I would have to take another semester of electives as they would not let me in the school of business since my GPA wasn't high enough. If I could get my GPA up where it needed to be, then I could get in. I asked if they could make some kind of concession since I had been dealing with so much. I knew if everything stayed consistent, I wouldn't have a problem getting the GPA up; but I also knew that with all the stuff happening, it was also a big if. They refused, and I thought it was too expensive to take another semester of classes I didn't need on a chance that I could get in the school of business. I went ahead and took a summer class that I needed and decided to put the education on a back burner for a while.

During this time, we would go to church on Sunday and then go for what we jokingly called our buffet dinner. After church, we would go pick up groceries so I wouldn't have to make another trip and so we could save gas. In those days, the stores would put out many samples, and you could almost have a meal from the samples in each store. Well, we did. The children would take as many samples as they could, and by the time we left the two stores I usually shopped at, they would have their dinner. I hated doing it but was thankful for the food and that it did help save some on groceries.

Along the Front Range, they require emission testing every year, and it came time for me to have the testing done. I took the car in for the testing, and the mechanic tested it, commenting he couldn't understand how it passed given the condition the car was in. I told him it was prayer and God that was keeping it together. He commented, "It must be."

My son who had been in the navy had been discharged and decided to stay at my mom's. One night I received a collect call that he was going to end his life. I knew I had to keep him on the phone, or I would lose him, but I also knew I couldn't afford the collect call. I was talking to him and praying in the spirit all the time for God to send someone to keep him from doing it. He finally disconnected the call. I immediately got on the phone to the church, requesting prayer, and then called the police where my mother lived. While I waited, I cried and prayed. It was about an hour, and I received a call from the police saying they had located him. I praised God for intervening and keeping him safe.

A friend helped me get a job with her husband at a drive-in as an assistant manager in training. I enjoyed the work, and he was wonderful to work for. He worked with me so I could have Sunday off to go to church, and things seemed to be going really good for a change.

I had worked there when another job opportunity opened up. A new family-owned grocery store was opening, and they were hiring. I had told the manager I was applying for the job, so after the interview, I came back, and we discussed it. Very seldom did I feel comfortable enough to discuss anything like that with a man, and now I realize the confidence I had in him. We weighed the pros and cons, and he felt like I would be better off taking the other job as it was allowing me possibilities for advancement, while working with him, I wouldn't be able to advance until he quit. I accepted the job and gave notice.

They had agreed that I could have every other Sunday off; it was more pay and more hours, plus possible overtime. The store was exciting, and I was in the bakery department. I began to realize some of the problems ahead when the manager of all the bakeries had to get a calculator out to divide $0.99 in half. The bakery store manager was a delight to work for and with. She maintained that distance where you had a professional relationship, but you were still friends. We would talk and laugh as we worked when we didn't have customers.

Suddenly, some strange things started happening. I came to work one day, and one of the young girls was working the floor alone during one of our busiest times. I asked what had happened, and she said they had walked our coworker to the door. The coworker had been with them for almost twenty years. She was really efficient and pleasant to work with. Her crime was she had purchased a doughnut and rang it up herself because the deli department was busy, and it was against company policy.

My manager was next. They fired her, saying she hadn't paid for a cup of coffee she had gotten. Later, she told me they had told her to write me up, and she told them she couldn't find anything to write me up on. They replaced her with a woman from one of the other stores. We referred to the new manager as the Amazon woman. She was very tall and big built. In reality, since I was the assistant manager, I should have been the next one in line, but I wasn't. What was interesting was they had me train her. Had I not been a Christian and wanted to do what was right before God, I could have really had fun with that. She had been there for a month, and I had four of my employees quit and most not even giving notice. She thought nothing of cussing you out in front of customers and putting you down because you didn't do something the way she thought you should.

One morning things were really busy, and I hadn't been able to get things in the cases like usual. She came into work and was belittling me in front of the customers and accusing me of coming in late and not getting right to work. I had a call come in for a special order, and I was trying to get all the details, with her putting me down in the background. I got off the phone and went to put the order where we kept them to be turned in, and she just about hit me in the head with a bakery tray. I was shocked myself, but I took off my apron and started to put it away. She wanted to know where I was going, and I told her I was done.

One of the women in the store told me to go talk to the store manager and see what could be done. That was the best advice I could have gotten for the situation. I talked to the store manager. He informed me they couldn't fire her as they had a contract with her, but he would see if he could get me into one of the other stores.

He wasn't able to, but because of trying to resolve the problem, I was able to get unemployment benefits through them.

I was going south on a street in the community we were living in and was at the intersection of Shields and Mountain. The light turned red, so I was sitting there, waiting for it to turn green, listening to Christian radio. I believe it was James Dobson speaking, but he made a comment that has stuck with me through the years. He said, "You see these little old ladies that are angry with life and always condemning every one and being very critical. They made a decision in their forties that life had done them wrong and allowed it to make them bitter. You can decide to let it make you better or bitter." I was in my forties, and I was becoming very bitter because of all that was happening. My ex-husband would have me get things for the baby, saying he would pay me back but would never reimburse me. Some of my daughter's friends were telling her I wasn't treating her right, and I was always being told I should kick her out and pursue my own life instead of what was best for her and the baby. I will be the first to tell you I made a lot of mistakes, but I did try to respect the fact it was her baby and to allow her to make the decisions for the baby. It is a hard line to walk when you are responsible for both of them. I always said they haven't written a book on single parenting a single parent.

That day, I sat there and cried out to God, asking Him to remove the bitterness and help me make this a stepping stone to become a better person instead of becoming bitter. I think it must have been an extralong light, or it changed a couple of times, but no one was behind me, so God could do His work in me. It always amazes me how God always works that out.

My second youngest son had gotten a job at a pizza place and was working evenings. I had been telling the children for some time that it felt like we had a loose wheel. They just laughed at me, saying I was being paranoid. This particular night, I was going to pick up my son from work on a very cold midnight. When I turned the corner after stopping at the stoplight in old town, it felt like I had a flat tire. I pulled into the first open parking spot, which happened to be a handicapped spot, to check the tire. I got out of the car. After further inspection, the tire was not flat but was at an angle. I didn't think it was safe to go ahead and drive it but wanted to make sure.

I had parked right in front of a Cajun Café, so I prayed for God to send someone who could help me. As the customers would come out, I would ask them if they knew anything about cars and kept being told they didn't. Finally, one person came out and said he would get the owner of the café to see if he could help me. He came out, looked at the car, and informed me I needed to call a taxi. I mentioned to him my situation and that I didn't have funds for a taxi. He said not to worry about it as he would pay for the taxi to go pick my son up and take the two of us home. He also said not to worry about being in a handicapped spot as he would take care of it if I promised to get the car moved within the next couple of days. Had I or the children been going down the highway, we would have lost the wheel, and who knows what would have happened? I know God had me at the right place so that nothing serious happened to the children, me, or the car, and I was giving Him praise for it.

My second eldest son had a friend who worked for a towing company, so I called him to see if he could help me. He checked with his boss and was able to get the car and tow it home for me. I had no idea what I was going to do for parts or anything else other than I knew we needed the car. My daughter had to be able to get the baby to day care so she could go to school. Had it not been for the baby, they all could have walked to school, and I could have caught the bus close to work and walked the rest of the way. The day care was quite a distance away. I let the church know that I wouldn't be to church and why. They said if someone could fix the car, they would pay for the parts. My two eldest sons had enough training in the military, so they could take care of the repairs the following weekend.

Eventually, the youngest child decided to move down with his dad. The other two decided they were moving out, and since they were eighteen and over, it was their decision. I gave up the housing we were in. I don't know if I could have stayed or not, but I felt since I really didn't need a three-bedroom by myself, it was better for me to give it up for someone who needed it. I went from a house full of children and a grandchild to nothing within a matter of weeks. A friend opened her home to me for a short while. Her mother-in-law was coming from New York, so I needed to find another place to stay.

I did finally find a really nice one-bedroom apartment in the north part of town. Most of the residents were single women, and we pretty much watched out for one another. There had been a person held up a couple of blocks from the apartment house, and they stole a Bronco jacket. I looked out the window, and there was a man standing on the corner, smoking. He was there for two days, and finally, I called the police because it was starting to concern me. It turned out to be an undercover cop. He changed his position after that.

I had felt led to write a letter to the editor of the paper. This was when the LGBT movement was just starting to surface. I had been doing a lot of reading from psychologists about the research concerning gay people. The paper never published it, but after sending it, I got a very frightening experience of spiritual warfare. I woke up in the middle of the night, and it was like I was being strangled, and I was paralyzed. I had enough presence of mind to start trying to call out the name of Jesus. At first, nothing would come out, but I kept saying it in my mind. Finally, I was able to say it out loud; and with each time I said it, the stranglehold on my neck would loosen. I knew it was demonic as there was no physical body there. When I was finally able to move, I got up and anointed all the window frames, doorframes, and outlet covers with oil and prayed protection over myself. I do have to admit it took me a few days to conquer the fear of going to sleep. I praise God for the scriptures Isaiah 26:3 ("You will keep in perfect peace him whose mind is steadfast, because he trusts in you") and Psalm 91:5 ("You will not fear the terror of night, nor the arrow that flies by day").

The landlord decided to let his granddaughter and her husband have the apartment next to me. The whole atmosphere of the apartment complex changed when they moved in. They were smoking pot and were always having parties. I tried talking with the landlord about it, but he let me know nothing was going to change, so I started looking for something else.

I don't know if it was the same Elizabeth Jacobs or another one who suddenly came into my life during this time. I still have not met this woman, but I received a call at work from a collection agency. They called me at work saying I had written a check to a flower shop that wasn't any good. I told them I had not written a check to any flower shop. They called me a liar and demanded payment. I asked them how they got my number. They said the number they had for her had been disconnected, so they got mine out of the phone book. I told them I had had that number for a long time, and I did not know that person. Needless to say, I wasn't the nicest to them since they were trying to make me responsible because I had the same name, and they had gotten my number out of the phone book.

Then I got a call late at night from a young boy. I answered the phone, and he said, "Mom, this is Brian." I told him I didn't have a son named Brian. Later, I realized how heartbreaking that must have been. I explained he must have gotten a wrong number and asked who he was trying to reach. He informed me he was trying to contact Elizabeth Jacobs. That really bothered me and just broke my heart. It took me a while to get over that.

I took my shoes to the shoe repair, and when I went to pick them up, they asked which Elizabeth Jacobs I was. They told me she was a tech person, which also raised my concerns as it seemed as though she was stalking me.

I went to the bank, and they pulled up a file, but it was hers, not mine. Then I received a call from the hospital, and it was on my answering machine when I got home after work on a Friday night. I was concerned that it might be my second youngest as I had found out he was having some kidney problems again. The hospital said they didn't have anyone registered by his name in the hospital. Finally, on Monday, I was able to find out what it was about when they transferred me to the bookkeeping department. They were trying to locate her concerning an uncollected bill. I was feeling that was too much to be coincidental.

I received a call late one night to have the pastor on the phone. He said the office administrator had quit without notice, and he was wondering if I would be interested in the position. He told me what they were offering and told me to pray about it. I told him I didn't need to pray about it. I had been praying that God would give me a job I hadn't applied for since I was tired of putting in the applications and dealing with the rejections. With what they were offering, it would be about the same as what I was making at the present time without all the commuting on the roads that were many times more hazardous in the winter months. Since I had worked for him at a previous church, I knew what kind of employer he was and was excited be working back with him again.

I finally found something, and the price was really good. My pastor had told me about it, and he knew the people who had lived there. They were moving out, and as a result, I got a jump on it before it was advertised. It was close to downtown and very quiet. My youngest decided to move back up in the area, and I was excited about that other than he told me he had gotten into some trouble and could be facing jail if they caught him. I told him to turn himself in as he couldn't run forever, but he chose not to.

Some strange things started happening at the apartment, and it was obvious someone was getting in the apartment when I wasn't there. I always locked the door, but the lock wasn't a very good one and was very easy to pop. God hadn't healed my eyes yet, so I was wearing contacts. I would go to get my contact lens solution to find them in a different spot each time.

One night I went to go to bed to find toenails between the sheets. Another time, my bar soap was standing between some bottles on my stand in the bathroom. One night I woke up because I heard a noise under the bedroom window. Someone was muttering outside the window. Another time, the man who lived in the basement apartment at the far end of the building knocked, wanting to borrow some sugar. I talked to the landlord about it. He said he would get a new lock but never did. I talked to him about what was going on, only to be informed that the man trying to borrow sugar was handicapped and was probably the one doing it, but he couldn't evict him because of his handicapped status. He suffered from insomnia. I found out later from one of the youth in the youth group that he was also a sex offender.

I called the police, and even though they never came and investigated it, they said they were pretty sure who it was and would keep a close eye on the apartment. I would come home from work, and he would plant himself in the middle of the sidewalk right in front of me and would try to start a conversation. I tried to be polite, but I didn't feel comfortable around him.

I started going back to college again. I was working at the church and going to college both full time. I had talked with the advisers at a different college, and they said there would be no problem signing off so I could take the classes I needed in the college of business. I was registered and ready to go.

This is the way I started out that semester. I came home, and there was a message from my youngest son but no details. I started calling the children to see if I could find out why he had called. Finally, one of them called me back saying word on the street was he had an accident; and since there was a warrant out for his arrest, he was in jail. They found out where his truck was, and I'm not sure who it was, but some of the family was able to get it off the street. Thankfully, he was not hurt, and there wasn't very much damage to his truck.

The church had asked me to do a volunteer handbook at the request of the insurance company on guidelines to protect our children. The board had also decided to have criminal checks done on all new volunteers. We had no more than completed the criminal checks when a woman in the church became disgruntled and decided to destroy one of our van drivers and also the church. Even though his criminal check had come back with no suspicious activity, she decided to report that he had gotten involved with one of the girls on the van. This man's fiancée was always with him, and they had become friends of the girl's family, but we weren't responsible for his actions with the family. Anyway, she decided to report it, and we were going through all kinds of investigations. We were praying hard about this as we knew what it would do to the church, and even the mother said this man was innocent. This was also going on during this problem with my son. We had gathered for prayer before going to court, and God miraculously intervened as we received a call that the case had been dropped for lack of evidence. I had also received a call about someone very close being molested, and because the parent was having trouble dealing with it, they wanted me to be there for them in court.

I received a call from my daughter sobbing uncontrollably, and I had trouble understanding her. Finally, she calmed down enough that I was able to find out what had happened. She had been to a party. A young man who was like one of my sons and had spent a lot of time at the house had also been to the party. He had been murdered just a half hour after she had been visiting with him. He was one of those kids who was always full of life and had a very inquisitive mind. From what I was told, one of the women at the party said she was afraid to walk home by herself, so he offered to walk her home. They got to the door, and he opened the door for her to be met by her husband with a shotgun in his hands. He shot this young man in the face, and he died on the spot.

With all that going on, at the end of the semester, I went in to see if I could drop down to part-time student. I was so thankful that they decided to work with me. At the end of that year, I decided to totally put school on the back burner indefinitely.

I started working with the youth and loved it. The first time I was asked to take their Sunday school class, I refused. I felt like I had done so poorly raising my children since none of them were living for the Lord that I wasn't qualified to teach them. God really got on my case about it and told me I had raised them right, but they had a choice, and they chose not to live for God. I finally told God that if the position opened up again, I would take it. Anyone who has walked with God very long knows if you tell God something like that, it isn't very long until the position will open up again. I took the Sunday school teacher position.

It wasn't very long when they asked me to work with another man doing the youth. I have to say those were probably some of the most enjoyable years of my life. I seldom ordered curriculum but sought God on what He wanted me to teach and did the preparation. They also had it that the fourth Sunday night of the month was youth night, and the youth had the service. I would encourage them to direct dramas and preach. There were a number of times when the ones who had volunteered to preach would come to me and say they weren't getting anything, so I would do the preaching. When that happened, God had usually already given me something to minister on. I always tried to encourage the youth to step into their calling as much as I could, so I only planned on ministering when none of them would step up to do it.

As the office manager, I was privileged to take part in a lot of the things that went on in the church, and I loved it. They considered me as part of the staff, so I was asked to visit the sick, pray for the ones who stopped in, and if the pastors weren't there was allowed to counsel also.

We had a revival with intercessory prayer, and that was such a wonderful time. I had never been drunk in the spirit before, and one time in prayer, God came down in such a powerful way that I could not stand. I dropped to the floor in a heap. When I got up, I was drunk in the spirit. We would take the intercessors out to eat after the prayer session, and I was so drunk that I had trouble ordering and an even harder time writing the check. The pastor finally ended up writing the checks for the meals. This happened on a Wednesday, and every time I would pray, the rest of the week, I would get drunk all over again. Poor pastor was so kind and understanding about it. He could have been very embarrassed, but he would just smile and continue with things that needed done. It was quite a challenge to count the offerings and type up the bulletin for the rest of the week. I look back and see all the healing that started during that time of drunkenness. It was so good and refreshing.

During that revival, I was sitting, praying with my eyes closed, and suddenly started praying differently, and my hands went out in front of me. I heard some motion on the floor in front of me but didn't know what it was. I kept praying and was finally able to open my eyes a little, and here was this very tall woman writhing like a snake in front of me with her hands over her heart, saying, "No, no." At that time, I was still new in demonic possession, but I did realize when I started praying so authoritatively that I was taking authority over a demon that was in her, and she was trying to keep it from leaving.

I asked God later what was going on. I felt God was telling me that she had sold her soul to the devil and believed that if that demon left, it would take her life as it went. God told me that Satan did not have that power, and if she had not refused, her next breath would have been a godly one. Later, I had a vision of her sitting in the middle of a circle of lit candles, saying chants. God told me she was trying to place curses on me as I was not afraid to stand up to her. I just rebuked the curses as I refused to walk in fear of the devil. I knew my God is more powerful.

I went to see my son in jail as much as I could and also tried to maintain contact. I have always told the children that if they got in trouble, I would not hire an attorney to get them off the hook. I would stand beside them, but they would have to pay the consequences for their actions. One day while talking to my son, he said they had put his friend's murderer in the same jail cell with him;

and needless to say, he was distraught about it. I tried calling to talk to someone about his placement, and they would not return my calls. Finally, I left a message that I did not have a problem with him paying for the crime he had committed, but I thought it was cruel and unjust punishment to be in the same prison cell with the person who had killed his best friend. If something wasn't done, they would be responsible for anything that happened. If something wasn't done about it, I would be trying to get an attorney. They never called back, but the next time I talked with him, the murderer had been moved.

After he was sentenced and while awaiting his placement, he had been transferred to the capital, which was closer, and I decided to go see him after my classes that day. I had just gotten a different car, and it was so cold that I was having trouble keeping the windshield clear enough to see to drive even though it was on full blast. The car had been an undercover car, so I was positive it was in good shape. I pulled up in front of the Colorado department of corrections and started to get out of the car. I looked at the dashboard, and it was covered with pot. I quickly wiped it off and could see the headlines, "Church secretary arrested in front of Colorado department of corrections for possession." Fortunately, no one was outside and saw me trying to wipe off the dashboard. I got in the building to find out I was at the wrong building. I breathed a sigh of relief and went to the right building to spend a little time with him.

When his time served was about to be completed, I received a call from the state confirming he was about to be released; and after a thorough investigation, they felt like I would be the best person for him to be released to. They wanted to know if I would be willing to let him come. I told them I would have to find a bigger place to live, but I would love to have him.

I started looking for another place to live and was wondering how I was going to be able to do it until he could get settled and find a job. I would get the paper, look at the rentals, and lay it aside as the prices were above what I felt I could afford. I was telling God I would really love to have a house as I was tired of apartment living, but then I would start rationalizing all the things I would need if I had a house.

One day I was looking at the paper, and here was a house for rent in the range I needed. I put the paper aside, thinking it was probably a dump or in a bad place of town. As I lay the paper aside, I once again told God, "But I would really like to have a house."

I heard this voice saying, "What's the problem with looking at this one?" I, of course, gave Him all the reasoning I just mentioned, but I really felt I was to check it out.

I called the landlord, and he hadn't rented it out yet. He was willing to let me come right over to look at it. I arrived at the house, and the minute he opened the door, I knew it was to be mine. It was perfect. The street was only about two blocks long, which meant the neighbor who was giving me problems couldn't find me by accident. The landlord said he would loan me the hoses for watering the grass, and he would take care of mowing the grass. I told him I had enough for the deposit or the rent, but I wouldn't have the money for both of them until the first of the month. He told me to go ahead and give him the deposit, and then I could give him the rent on the first when it would be due. To top it all off, he said I could start moving in immediately.

I set up a date to move, and the youth all came over and helped me move. God had provided my house, and it was even better than I had anticipated. For quite a while after that, people needing houses were calling me to pray for them to get a house, and God would always answer. God is so good.

I was there for about two years when I sensed God was telling me I was going to have another transition. I have to admit I was really struggling with it as things were going so well. In fact, I had never had them so good.

I had just finished taking the youth to the capital on a one-day mission trip. We had seen people give their hearts to the Lord. We had stopped at a fast-food place to debrief and were able to purchase a dinner for a homeless man and his friend. The one accepted Christ even though his friend made fun of him, and we were able to give him some contacts and a Bible to help him grow in the Lord.

I was already starting to make plans for the next mission trip on a reservation. I was so excited about what God was doing for the youth. The trip was exciting in itself. We had set a budget, and because of a person I had met at a Christian singles group, we were able to get everything under the budget. I told him what our budget was, and he was an assistant manager at a chain grocery store. When I picked up the food, I took my little Mazda, figuring it would all fit in it. I had to call my son and ask to use his pickup as I couldn't fit it in my car. We were able to take two vans. One was mostly filled with food and a couple of youth and driver, and the other one was filled with youth. God had provided above what we had even asked for. ("But my God shall supply all your need according to his riches in glory by Christ Jesus" [Philippians 4:19, KJV].)

God had been waking me up for about two weeks at around two in the morning, and I would feel the need to pray. I jokingly told someone, "I guess God was calling me to be the night watchman with him." After two weeks of this, my youngest son called at about two in the morning asking if I could come get him as he had a flat tire and didn't have a spare. I brought him home with plans that, the next day, we would get the tire fixed and put it back on his vehicle. We replaced it and got started down the road when I noticed he was pulling over. I stopped to find out what was going on, and he said the other tire was going flat.

Fortunately, we were close to a tire store, and they could replace it right away so I could get to work. The man surveyed the damage as he took the tire off and asked us where we had purchased the rim that the tire was on. I told him it had been on the vehicle and asked why he was asking. He said with the rim in the shape it was, it was a miracle that he didn't roll his vehicle; and if he had, he would probably have been killed. I thanked God for keeping His hand on my son and never again complained about being called to do night duty in prayer.

You can see why I was having trouble with the decision to move, but I knew I had to obey. I took a vacation in a neighboring state to visit one of my other sons, and all the way there, I was asking God where He wanted me. He was probably saying, *Would you just shut up and listen?* But thank goodness He is very patient. I finally realized He wanted me to move to the community I was going to visit. I came home and started making plans for my departure. I knew it wasn't going to be right away, but since I had to make sure my replacement would know what to do, I needed to make sure I had detailed instructions. They had already hired a youth pastor, and she was taking over those responsibilities. I did continue working some with the youth until she had transitioned into the position, and I continued teaching the teens.

I did tell God that if I was to move, I wanted to know my mother wouldn't be alone when she passed away and that my granddaughter would have someone to take her to church and wouldn't miss me too much since she had been with me a great deal. Also, it had to be okay with my son who was living in that community. I got home after being gone for two weeks, and my granddaughter hadn't even realized I had been gone. A lady at the church who lived close to them said she would take her to church when I moved. My son, when I said something, was ready to get some trailers and a crew and come get me. I had sensed I wasn't to move until May of the following year.

When I told the board I felt God was calling me somewhere else, their first response was "Who is he?" I told them it wasn't a he, and if they realized where I was going, they would know it was God. They did decide to give me a three-month severance pay, which I greatly appreciated.

I still remember the going-away party they gave me. They asked people to give me cards. If they wanted to give me money, that was fine, and I could put it on something I was wanting. When I read the cards, I cried. I had never realized how loved I was. I knew they cared, but because I had never known unconditional love, it had been hard for me to see how highly they thought of me and loved me.

I had wanted a certain picture that had been such an encouragement over the years and a Bible with a purple leather cover. The picture I wanted was no longer available as they had sold their last signed and numbered reprint. It was a Native American picture by Bill Jaxton of an Indian village and a cloud in the formation of a hand over the village. The story that accompanied it was that the Great Spirit would take care of them and protect them. Since they no longer had it, I decided on one that was similar in story. It was a picture of a white buffalo, and there were a pack of wolves, but the Great Spirit was protecting the buffalo. The story was he would provide for the pack in a different way. I still have both the Bible and the picture as they are very precious to me.

That May, my son came with some of his friends. They had a covered trailer for all my things and a trailer for the car as we didn't think that the car could make the trip. We loaded them up and headed for the community God had told me to move to. We were glad we had the covered trailer as it poured on us most of the way there. The place where my son lived was a big house, and his landlord had consented to my renting a room from him.

Chapter 10

We arrived and immediately unloaded the trailers. The room I was renting was so large that I was able to put most of my things in it. The only things we needed to store were the kitchen things. I quickly put things away and started trying to get the place cleaned up as best as I could.

Even though there were a lot of hard times, there was also a lot of growth in the Lord as He revealed and showed things to me. I loved that time of growth in Him.

When I first got there, every time I would go to church and they would open the altars for people to pray, I would go down, and I would be weeping like I had just lost a loved one. I thought it was stupid, and I couldn't figure out what was going on. Yes, I missed my children but not to that extent. I started asking God what was going on. He revealed to me a lot of the spiritual stuff that was going on in the church that was breaking His heart. I realized there were a lot of Jezebel spirits in operation there.

After getting settled, I started looking for work, and nothing was coming through. I decided to go to the college and see about getting enrolled for the fall term. The woman I spoke to said she would like to be my counselor, and since I had my records, we sat down and decided what classes I needed to take. She informed me that two classes I needed to take had started the day before, and she would enroll me into them. My first question was, "What will I do about the money as I haven't applied for any of the loans?" She informed me not to worry about it; we would go ahead and start the process and wait for the money to come in. She turned out to be my professor for a number of the classes I took through the summer.

I continued to submit résumés and was really getting discouraged as I knew I needed something. The day the severance pay ran out, I walked into the chamber of commerce and told them I was looking for work. They said they didn't have any openings, but I left my résumé there like I had done at all the other places I had applied. I got almost to the car when the office administrator came running out, saying they just remembered there was going to be some transitioning in the office as the director was taking a new position with the state, the office manager was going to take that position, and they were going to need someone to take the office manager position. They wanted to interview me, and I was hired on the spot. I would be working thirty-six hours a week, there were two part-time employees, and the chamber of commerce would work with me on my school schedule. I worked with the chamber until I graduated from college in December of 2000. It was quite a learning curve as I knew nothing about the community, let alone any of the functions of the chamber of commerce or the organizations under their umbrella. I have to admit I did love the challenge.

I had all these visions of things I was going to do for the Lord while I was there. I have to admit I didn't do any of them as I never had the funds to do so. I have many times felt like I should have just stepped out in faith to do them and trusted God to provide, but I didn't. I know that is the past, and there is nothing I can do other than ask God to forgive me and learn from it.

Doing devotions after I had moved there was really awesome as God was revealing so many things to me with confirmations. I read one morning in Matthew 13 about the sower, and some of the seed fell on hard soil, so the plant didn't get good rooting and soon died. The person planting didn't bring forth a harvest. I had remembered arguing with a woman because she said that her daughter had a hard heart, and she had to accept that she would not be saved because of this scripture. I told her I was not buying into that lie, and she got really upset with me. I told her my God was a God of miracles, and nothing was impossible with Him. For her to claim what she was claiming, she was saying that God wasn't God of the impossible. She argued that God allows man to decide. I told her God has the ability to change our want toos.

I asked God about this scripture as I do not want to believe that those teachings were right when God is all-powerful. He told me that those seeds could bring forth a harvest. I received a newsletter from a Christian organization. The article was about the hard soil and how a tree had been found growing above timberline in a rock. After investigation, they found the seed had evidently been dropped by a bird and fell in a crack in the rock. It had produced a root, and the root had found an underground spring that was watering the tree, allowing it to grow. I thought, *That'll preach.* I felt God was saying the underground spring was the Holy Ghost filling the hardened heart, allowing it to grow and mature in Him.

Also, I was reading in Joshua that the Israelites were getting ready to cross the Jordan River into the Promised Land. I had seen all these pictures in my youth of the priests walking on the beach into the gentle flowing water with the ark on their shoulders. For some reason, this day, the phrase "the waters were at flood stage" caught my eye. If you have ever seen a river at flood stage, it is not gentle flowing. The water is very turbulent. Then I felt I should look up what the Jordan River looked like when it wasn't at flood stage. I realized the priests were getting ready to step into a river with turbulent water with their most prized possession on their shoulders, not knowing if their next step was going to be a step down or a drop.

Even though I hadn't really thought of going into the ministry, I felt God was telling me that "Step into the Water" was what He wanted me to name the ministry He was giving me. At that time, I didn't realize what was ahead with a ministry name like that. It meant I got to be the forerunner to step into the water for the waters to part so I could minister to people and encourage them to grab hold of God's promises, trust Him, and step out to do His calling.

I did a number of prayer walks around the church, and I kept seeing this huge dragon over the church. I would pray, and the dragon would go down in size. When I would stop praying, the dragon would immediately grow back up to size. I asked God what I was doing wrong that I wasn't seeing it totally deflate and die. God told me I needed to pray for the arrows of my prayers to go between the scales as my prayers were hitting the scales and glancing off. Later, I received something that was telling about the scales on a dragon, and the only way you could kill one was to get in a position where the weapon would go between the scales and into the heart. If it didn't get between the scales, it would glance off. Once again, I had received a confirmation from God.

God also started revealing to me how to pray concerning the Jezebel spirits. I wasn't in a position where I could confront them, which I have learned, in many cases, is not wise. They will play the victim, get everyone to feel sorry for them, and get people to turn against you. I felt God directing me to pray for them to be constricted so they couldn't move or manipulate. I did see it working as God started exposing them.

Another situation I had was a friend suddenly started avoiding me. I asked her a couple of times if I had done something to offend her, and she always said no. When we would have a greeting time at church, she would always go away from me. One Sunday God showed me this demon sitting on her shoulder. I went over and gave her a great, big hug and quietly commanded the demon to leave. She said something, so I knew she felt something happen, and from then on, she was the same as she had always been.

I made the decision to go back to spend Christmas with my family even though the car was using oil. I wanted to see the children and also see Mom. Even though Mom never remembered me, I knew I needed to make sure she was doing well. She would always tell people I was her sister or her neighbor. She would always recognize and remember my brother, but I could never understand why she didn't know me.

I stopped to see her, and she had a sore on the temple area. I asked what had happened, and she said she had reacted to the permanent wave solution from a permanent they had given her. I knew that sometimes she did that, so I wasn't too concerned about it.

I went on to see the children and spend some time with them and then returned home, stopping to see Mom again on the way back. Since I was running low on gas, I stopped at a gas station to fill up, and this red car pulled up in the fueling area beside me. There were two couples in the car, and I jokingly said to the one fueling up that I was filling it up with oil and topping the gas, mentioning that it was using oil and that I hoped it would get me home. The man asked me where I was going, so I told him. He said they were going to a community close to there, and they would keep an eye on me to make sure I made it home okay. I went in to the station, paid for the gas, came out, and there was no one there. I looked all around, and I could not see a red car anywhere. As flat as that state was, I should have been able to see the car somewhere. I fumed for a little bit. How could they keep an eye out for me if they took off and left me? Later, I realized I had entertained angels unawares, and it was God just letting me know that He was watching over me as in Hebrews 13:2 (KJV): "Be not forgetful to entertain strangers, for thereby some have entertained angels unawares." I made it home without any problems.

When I got back, I started talking with a dealership that was a member of the chamber about trading cars. I had gotten to know one of the salesmen pretty well, and he had promised he would make sure I got a good deal. He found a car for me that they were saying was in good condition, so I traded. I was able to pay off the old car. I hadn't even had the car a month when I discovered I had some problems. I took it back to them, and they gave me a price. I didn't know what I was going to do as I didn't have that kind of funds, especially while making payments on it. He fought for me, and they decided they would do the repairs, and all I would have to do was pay for the parts. I accepted that.

That was how I started out that February. It was a month from hell, and I was so glad it didn't have twenty-nine days. Where I was renting, I was hearing rumors that the landlord hadn't been making his payments on the house and was losing it. That meant I was going to have to find another place to live. It did turn out that he had another place, which was the one he was losing, but I didn't know. Finally, I asked my son, and he told me it wasn't the one we were living in.

I went to write a check to pay for some things in a neighboring town, and they wouldn't accept it. All they would do was give me a number to call. I was so embarrassed as that had never happened to me before, and there had been a long line of people behind me. The manager took their time in coming, and people were getting impatient behind me. I knew I had money in the bank, so it shouldn't have been a problem. In the embarrassment, I forgot I had a credit card I could have used to pay for it, but it didn't even cross my mind.

I got home and called the number, only to be told that my driver's license number was used for identification for a check written before I had even moved into the state. I told the person it couldn't have been mine and explained to him I didn't have a license to drive in that state at that time. He was very rude and informed me I was lying and that I had changed the driver license. I don't know where he got that idea because if I was going to use it to write bad checks, I sure wouldn't have it changed using the same number I was using to write them with. There were all kinds of hoops I had to jump through to get that straightened out but finally did get the situation resolved.

After paying off the car I traded in, I never received title. I suddenly wasn't getting my bank statements either, so I started calling around, trying to find out what was going on with both of them. I was informed that they had both been mailed out, and I should have gotten them. I had asked my youngest son if they were coming to him since I had cosigned a note for him. He said he hadn't seen them. He asked his roommates, and they hadn't seen them either. I called the bank again, and they kept insisting they had mailed them to me. Finally, I asked where they sent them. I had never heard of the address and told them so. I did call and check with my son to find that it was his new address. I asked why they had changed the address to my things. I was informed that when they changed my son's address, they changed the address on everything.

I asked what they were going to do about the title. They informed me they weren't going to do anything. I would need to apply to the state for a lost title and pay for it. I said, "So you're telling me that you lost the title to my car because you sent it to the wrong address and now I am supposed to pay for your error?" They informed me that was right. I told the dealership what was going on, and they said they would take care of it for me, which I greatly appreciated.

Almost every day that month, something similar to those things happened. It was unreal. I told someone on the phone, trying to get something taken care of, "I'm sure glad it is the last day of the month as I am more than ready to be done with February and to have a new start." I had another February like that a few years later, so from then on, when February would arrive, I would start rebuking the enemy and breaking off curses. I was doing anything I thought or felt like I needed to do so it wouldn't happen again.

I had the opportunity of renting a house with two sisters and jumped on the opportunity as I knew the owner and knew I wasn't going to face concerns of being without a place to live again. It wasn't the greatest situation as my bed was in the laundry room, but it worked out until I graduated. The girls decided they wanted to move to a different place so they would be alone, so I started looking for something else. It was December, and I would be graduating. I made plans to celebrate my graduation and made all the decorations. I was really proud of how it looked. I was also proud of the fact that I had been invited to join the honor society for nontraditional students. My second youngest son, with his two girls, came to join me on the celebration. After the graduation, he headed home. I worked until the week of Christmas and headed back home to see the rest of the children and make sure Mom was doing okay.

I had mentioned to one of the men who belonged to the chamber of commerce that I needed a place to live. He said he had a one-bedroom apartment that was available for rent. The price was right, so I had my place to live. It was very spacious, which I loved, and it also gave me plenty of room to put up my Christmas decorations.

The trip home went well. On the way back, I stopped by the care center to visit Mom. She still had the sore on her temple, only now it was about the size of a quarter. I asked the nurse about it and was told they had tried everything on it, and it wouldn't heal. It looked to me like skin cancer, which was one of the easiest to treat. I asked why she hadn't been to the doctor and was told they were going to take her the following week. I was very concerned as our family is full of cancer.

After I got home, I called the nursing home to find out what the doctor had said. I was informed they didn't think they needed to bring her in and implied that because she was elderly, we should just ignore it and let it go its course as she really had no value. I was furious. I told them I was reporting it to the state, which I did. By the time the state got there to check it out, the sore was completely healed.

I stopped at my former neighbor's for the night before continuing on home. She allowed me to sleep on the top bunk of the bunk beds she had in her daughter's room. I don't know what I did, but getting down that morning, I knocked my feet out from under me on the ladder going down. I did catch myself, so I didn't hit my head on the corner of the desk, but I did something to my right arm. It was a really strange thing as I couldn't really put a place on where it hurt. It seemed to always be moving around. I would pray for the spot that hurt, and it would quit hurting, but it would start hurting somewhere else. Finally, I asked God what was going on. He told me it was a migrating infirmity and that I needed to take authority for it to stop moving. When I did that, it quit moving around, and then I was able to pray for the spot, and it quit hurting.

One of my friends came over, and we got everything packed and moved to the new apartment. I had also told the chamber of commerce that unless I could get an increase in pay, I would be quitting. By then, the two part-time people had quit, and I was handling everything by myself. I wasn't asking for double the pay even though I was doing double the work, but I was asking for time and a half of what I had been getting. They decided to not give me the raise, so I moved on.

The next job was a data entry job, and I was really enjoying it. Suddenly, people who had been visiting with me during breaks wouldn't have anything to do with me. The supervisor called me in, saying there had been complaints about me smelling and commenting that I needed to take a shower more often. I was brokenhearted as I did take showers every day and always tried to make sure I was clean. I stayed for a little longer until I could find something else and then put in my resignation.

The day I gave them my resignation, a woman hurriedly walked past my cubicle, putting a sticky note on my desk in front of me. I read the note, and it said I should meet her in the basement bathroom and make sure no one saw me. I didn't even know where the basement bathroom was. I went down, looked around, and found it. I entered, and the woman peeked out the door to make sure I hadn't been followed. She was the head of the QA section. Her first comment was "You actually have pants on." I told her that I did own slacks, but I didn't wear them often. She told me then that some of what she called the mafia had threatened anyone who was friendly to me. They had made derogatory statements because I always wore dresses and were trying to destroy me. She said that she was sorry I was being treated that way. She also commented that even though I was a little slower because of being new, my work was excellent and very seldom had to be corrected at all. She also said I didn't deserve to be treated like they had treated me. It was obvious she was fearful of them, and she said that as long as I was working there, she would not associate with me. After I was no longer employed there, we did see each other occasionally.

I had loaned the chamber of commerce my Christmas decorations for the office since I wasn't using them in the house I had been living in. I had planned on getting them around the middle of January when I got back home and the Christmas season was over. Before I got them picked up, there was a fire at the chamber of commerce. The director just took all my Christmas things out and threw them in the trash. I had silk purple poinsettias, a number of Christmas floral arrangements, Native American ornaments, and a number of Nativity scenes. Fortunately for me, a friend worked in the same office with the federal housing and rescued most of them for me. They were things that could not be replaced easily. I couldn't believe anyone would do something like that without even talking to me about what I wanted to do with them.

After the data entry job, I had a sales job selling online programs to schools. I had only been working there for a short time when I called Mom to talk with her, and all she would do was moan and say, "Help me." She was always trying to get me to come and get her so I could take care of her. I knew that it was not something I could do as I needed to work, and I couldn't be with her all the time. Plus, she was bigger than I was, and I knew I couldn't take care of her the way she needed to be. When she had been with my brother, she had gotten to the point where she refused to do anything for herself, including bathroom duties, and had my brother helping her with them. As a result, I called my brother to see how she responded to him. She would always be good with him. He reported she was responding the same way to him. I called my other brother and left him a message.

I went ahead and went to my friend's graduation while I was waiting. While I was at the graduation, I got the call from my other brother and told him what was going on. He said he felt I should come. I told him I couldn't make two trips because of the new job and the finances. He said he would pay for the second trip if I needed to make one. I went to the apartment and packed to go for at least the weekend. I stopped at my brother's, and we went on to see Mom together, leaving my car at his place. We got to the care center, and her feet were black from gangrene with purple streaks clear up to her waist. I was furious, and by then, she was pretty much unresponsive.

My brother and I sat and sang to her as that was the only thing that seemed to calm her. My brother went back to his house, and I stayed with Mom. My eldest brother said he wouldn't be able to come as he had an important doctor appointment on Monday and could not miss it. They were doing a biopsy on him for lung cancer. By Monday, I had assessed the situation and knew Mom wasn't going to make it much longer. It had been strange as when I got her Mother's Day card, I always purchased her birthday card and sent them at the same time since they were close. I kept feeling like I wasn't going to need the birthday card, but I got it and sent it anyway. This was the week after Mother's Day.

I knew my eldest brother was to be the executor over Mom's things, and if anything happened to him, I was to be the one to make the decisions. I thought in the event of his death, it would roll over to me. I called him and told him what was going on and asked him to check and see if I would be authorized to make the decisions. Plus, she had told us all the arrangements had been made with the mortuary. It wasn't too long before I had a call from my brother saying the way it had been drawn up was that if he wasn't in a capacity to make those decisions, they would roll over to me. I felt guilty calling around to find out information concerning her death when she was still alive but knew I needed to know what I was going to need to do. I called the mortuary to find there really weren't any arrangements made other than the money that had been set aside for her burial.

That week was a hard week, but God did so many wonderful things. I saw God restoring the relationship between my elder brother and myself where it had been strained for a number of years. I didn't want to leave Mom, and it turned out that one of my classmates' parents were at the nursing home. He had Alzheimer's, and she had moved in also just to be close to him. She came to see Mom as she had heard I was there. She told me to go get something to eat and get some rest. She would stay with Mom while I was gone.

I called the classmate who had bought Mom's house and asked if I could take a shower at their place. (We had joked that there was a contingency clause in the purchase that anytime I needed a place to stay when I was back, I could stay with them.) His wife said she would come get me and that I was more than welcome to take a shower there. I finished with the shower, and she had fixed me some lunch. She had also found me a change of clothes since all my clothes were in my car at my brother's. After I ate, she took me back to the care center.

I sang to Mom all night until my voice was almost gone. The hall would be lined with people listening to me sing. The only thing that seemed to help was my singing the old hymns to her. She did come around a little bit once, and I told her that heaven was waiting. I was sure God had a shovel and hoe waiting for her to take care of His gardens and told her the flowers were the largest and most beautiful she had ever seen. She opened her eyes and looked at me as though to ask, *Do you really think so?* And she lay back down.

I also felt she needed to forgive Dad for the way she felt toward him. I knew she still had bitterness toward him, and I knew she couldn't get into heaven with unforgiveness in her heart. I led her in a prayer of forgiveness as I know the sense of hearing is the last to go. I also realized she wasn't going to live much longer and told the nurses to let the people who wanted to tell her their goodbyes that they were welcome to come in and spend some time with her. I started asking God what was keeping her as my brothers and I had all released her to go.

God reminded me of a woman Mom had taken under her wing when both her parents had died. I called her daughter to get her phone number as I had lost contact with her. The daughter said she would let her Mom know and have her call Mom's room. Her mom did call, and we put the phone up to Mom's ear, but there was no response. That evening, the daughter came with her husband to see Mom. She talked to Mom for a short while and then went to leave. My brother and I were standing in the hall talking with them, when my brother said he was going back to check on Mom. She was breathing her last breath. We knew that this daughter had been the key to Mom's feeling released to go home. It turned out that, over the years, she would mistake the daughter for her mother as their voices sounded alike.

When it came to making the decisions concerning the funeral, we were all in agreement. It was all about "What do you think Mom would want?" There was such harmony that I knew it was God. Mom had wanted me to play for her funeral and for my brother and me to sing. We were able to work together in harmony, and later after listening to the video of the funeral, I was amazed as you would have thought we had been singing together regularly. We would change parts without even signaling each other, and the transitions were smooth.

Things did get pretty interesting for a while, but I finally got a little stern and held my ground. I had called the family and let them know Mom was dying, but after she died, I was shocked at some of the stuff that happened. My uncle in California informed me it was too expensive for him and his son to fly out at that short notice and wanted me to delay the funeral so they could drive out. My uncle was not in that good health but was determined to come to the funeral. My cousin thought we should delay to a different time as his wife couldn't come because she had a client to take care of the day of the funeral. The mortician said he couldn't do it on the weekend as he had something scheduled. My daughter said she was coming, and she was having contractions. I was envisioning ambulances arriving in the middle of the funeral because my daughter was having her baby and my uncle having a heart attack. I had already been off work for a week, and even though I had just started the job, they had said they would give me grievance pay for the three days as was in the employee manual.

My brother and I discussed it and decided we were not making changes for them. My eldest brother wasn't able to come and actually ended up going back to the hospital at the same time the funeral dinner was being served. The place where they had done the biopsy in his lung had not sealed allowing the air to go out through the hole One of my nephews had stayed with him, and the other one had brought my sister-in-law down for the funeral. We were praising God that my eldest brother had not been there alone and thankful that my nephew was there to get him help.

My eldest had called his biological father, and of course, the others had told their father. Both my exes were there for the funeral. Some people asked me how I felt about it. I told them, "If they felt like they needed their fathers there, then I didn't have a problem with it as, with me having to take care of the music and stuff, I really wasn't going to have much time to be there for them." The only problem that arose was a woman who wanted to talk to me about some personal things. She got upset because people kept coming over to talk with me and interrupting her conversation. She made a rude comment about me not having time for her and left. I have never seen her again.

My brother and I decided that, so the residents would have their opportunity to remember her, we would have a memorial service for her at the care center. We allowed them to tell stories about things they remembered of her, and we also sang some songs. The staff had some refreshments. They all seemed to enjoy it and thanked us for doing it. The staff even commented about how rare it was for families to do something like that or to allow residents to come in and say their goodbyes. My thought was that she had been a businesswoman for many years in the community and well thought of, so why shouldn't they have that opportunity?

My second eldest son left right after the funeral as he had committed to go on a trail ride with some of his friends in a different state. For weeks, God had been waking me up in the night to pray for Him but wasn't sharing with me about why. I headed home as soon as we had everything completed. It wasn't long after arriving home that I received a call from my second eldest saying he had an accident and totaled his truck. His friend said the truck was so bad that it made him sick to his stomach when he saw it. The officer who investigated the accident asked why he was still there. My son asked him to explain. The officer informed him he had just recently investigated an accident that wasn't nearly as bad, and the driver was killed in the accident. My son told him, "It's because I have a praying mother."

I was at the sales job for two years. Overall, I did enjoy the job. They made some crazy decisions, and I would usually tell them my philosophy on the decisions. I always tried to do it nicely as a means of discussion. Some of the employees thought I was going to get us all fired, but the owners knew me on a first-name basis and always seemed to respect me even though they didn't change their plans.

One situation was they decided to lay a bunch of people off as it was the summer months. Since we dealt with schools, we weren't making very many contacts. They had told us to continue contacting the schools when everyone knew no one is in the schools during the summer. I started out by telling them I had disobeyed their orders as I didn't like wasting their time and not getting any results. As a result, I was calling the districts, private schools since they were usually in connection with a church, and the state departments of education. I was getting people on the phone and some responses. Also, it really wasn't a good time to be laying people off as we needed to be gearing up for when the schools started up again. If we let the people go, then we would need to retrain a whole new crew in another month. Calling the private schools, districts, and states would give people contacts to work on for the month before the schools opened.

Another decision they made was they would pay the outside sales representative for every sale the inside person made in their district. I probably wasn't as nice about that one as, to me, it was stupid. I let them know if they did something like that, most outside sales representatives would do nothing and let the inside salespeople do all the work. It didn't take too long for them to change that as most of the outside salespeople weren't doing anything.

During my lunch, God would have me sit on a bench on the street and pray for the community. One time I saw the little Scrubbing Bubbles brushes going down the street, sweeping. It looked so funny that I burst out laughing. After I had prayed for a long time and hadn't seen anything happening, I told God I didn't think I was accomplishing much, and I was going to stop. A couple of days later, there was a news truck in front of the building and all kinds of policemen wandering around. Then America's most wanted showed up. It turned out a young man had come to meet one of the businessmen for a relationship, and they refused to let him leave when he requested. He had finally gotten away and gone to the police. I never doubted my prayers after that. I know, more than likely, I wasn't the only one praying, but it made me aware of the importance of listening to those promptings of the Holy Spirit.

While there, I started having problems with perfumes. If someone sprayed any perfumed odor killers, I would start coughing and choking. Then it got to the point that if someone came in with heavy perfume on, I would start coughing and have to go home. One of the supervisors actually got to the point that when they came in with perfume on, she would send them home to take a bath before they came back. I appreciated her concern but also felt sorry for the ones she was being so rough on.

I would go in to donate blood, which I had done for years, and my blood pressure was at stroke level. I didn't know what was going on as I was still eating the same, and there wasn't anything new going on that would have been causing severe stress. I didn't realize I had developed what was called a chemical intolerance, with perfumes being the main culprit, and that was one of the signs of greater problems from it.

The business changed ownership, and I have to say I really liked the new owner and thought he could possibly do something with the company. I was sensing God was telling me to quit, so I prayed about it for a while. God gave me the date that was to be my last day, so I went in to tell my supervisor. He came back stating they didn't want me to quit as they had plans for me with the company as they expanded to the southern part of the United States. I told him I would pray about it over the weekend and give him the answer on Monday. I still kept feeling like I was to quit at the end of March, and the first week after I quit, I was to spend the time praying for the community.

I had felt that God wanted me to have the college students who came to church on Sunday for a homemade dinner, and then if they wanted, they could stay, and we would pray. One of the college students' parents had come earlier in the year, and we had a wonderful prayer time together. I received a call later from the pastor as some people had some concerns about them. The young woman's parents had connections with International House Of Prayer in Kansas City. We had a wonderful prayer time, but I do have to admit they acted a little different from what I was used to. I feel that the concern was the people of the church had never seen anyone with that kind of fire. Anyway, the one young lady said they wanted me to go to International House Of Prayer with them for a special meeting that weekend, and she was going also. Then her mother wanted to know if it was okay if she came back and stayed with me for a week as God was telling her to come pray for the community. Once again, there was a confirmation on what I was to do the week after quitting the job.

International House Of Prayer was a wonderful experience. I was so excited to see how they were working with the children, teaching them to pray and believe God for the miracle. It was also so beautiful seeing the men dance in praise and worship to our Lord. I could hardly take my eyes off them as it was so beautiful to watch them. This was also the first time I experienced people laughing in the spirit. At first, I thought they were being disrespectful, and then God opened my eyes to understand they were enjoying the presence of God.

We returned home late and, the next morning, started making plans for how we were going to pray for the community. We were going to fast and pray for the community for the whole week. She informed me that I was praying and prophesying all night. I apologized for her not being able to get much sleep because of it, but she actually thought it was wonderful.

On Monday, we were to pray over the four corners of the community, placing a Popsicle stick with scripture references on it at each highway entrance and praying over the government buildings. The second day, we were going to pray over the schools. The third day, we were going to pray over the churches, and I don't remember what we were doing for the rest of the days. The first day went wonderful. The second day, we prayed around the grade school seven times about everything God told us to pray about.

The next school was the middle school. The mascot was a blue devil. We went around the school once, and as we started around the second time, I went to step up on a rock next to the building. It had snowed the night before and was really cold, so I was trying to be careful of my step but felt I was to make sure I had a good footing. I was just testing my footing when I heard a snap. I knew instantly I had broken my ankle. I was determined I could continue, but after one step, I realized I wasn't going on any more trips around the school. She offered to take me to the car, but I told her, "No, just help me to the flagpole, and I will stand there until you're finished, and then you can help me to the car." She finished and helped me to the car. I drove to the high school.

I knew I couldn't go around, so I sat in the car while she prayed around the high school. At one point, I was starting to get cold and thought I would start the car but was told by God that if she was doing it in the cold, the most I could do was partner with her in the cold. We finished and went back to the apartment for something hot to drink so we could head to the college that night. We did run down some crutches that I could use for a couple of weeks, and they were going to meet us at the college for the exchange. We had prayed for the ankle and believed for complete healing. I was using the crutches some, but I was also continuing to walk on it some without putting full weight on it. We had also picked up an ankle ACE bandage to help with the swelling and to support it.

We went to the college and prayed for it. We did walk around a couple of buildings but mostly stayed in one place and prayed. I was able to get the crutches, which did help in getting around some. We had joined some college students at the college, and they joined us in prayer.

The third day, we went to the churches and prayed outside them. The fourth day, we prayed over the businesses of the community but stayed at the apartment to do them and also went to a prayer meeting at the church. The fifth day was spent praying for the members of the community. The sixth day she spent trying to make sure things would be easy for me after she left, and then her husband came to pick her up. What a fabulous prayer time we had.

On Tuesday after she had gone back, the assistant pastor's wife called wanting to know if I could watch their girls as she needed to go out of town. I told her I would do it, but I really didn't think I could handle the baby with my ankle like it was. She said that would not be a problem as she could take the baby with her. The girls were really good, and I was thankful for that.

When she came to pick them up, I asked her to look at the bottom of my foot as I had noticed it was red like it was possibly burned. I didn't know if maybe I had burned it from the hot pad that I had been keeping on it or if I was reacting to the ACE bandage. She looked at it and told me to go to the doctor. I told her I didn't have insurance and money to pay for one. She thought I should get in right away and said she would take care of it as she wasted more money than it would cost. I went to the facility that she suggested, only to be informed they would not even touch it without my getting it x-rayed, and the X-ray department at the hospital was closed for lunch.

The physician's assistant recommended that I go to the neighboring town to get the X-rays rather than wait, so I got in the car and drove to that community. They took me and got me right in to the X-ray room. When the X-rays came back, they said they were glad they had taken them because of where my ankle had broken. They were recommending that I go to a specialist. If it wasn't set right, it would give me problems the rest of my life as it would affect the growth plate. (Since I was through growing, I really didn't see how that would matter but took their word for it.) I went to the specialist, and when they found out I had been walking on it for about a week and a half, they were totally surprised. The ankle did not need to be set as it was in perfect alignment. I knew it was God who had kept it from slipping out of place.

They put it in a boot and told me I wasn't to drive or put any weight on it whatsoever. I told them I had a problem as I had driven myself there, and I had no way of getting home. They did give their consent for me to drive as long as I kept the boot on until I got in the car without putting weight on it. Then I could take the boot off to drive home since it was my right ankle, and then when I got home, I was to put the boot back on and use the crutches to get into the house. They told me to come back in two weeks to see how it was healing, and I was not to be driving or walking on it during that time.

What a challenge those two weeks were. I sensed at first that God was telling me to stay in the house. I realized I had lost an earring, and it wasn't in the apartment, so I decided I would go check to see if it was in the car. That trip to the car was quite the trip. The crutches kept slipping out from under me, and I about fell a couple of times. The earring was just at the car door, so I picked it up and started back to the apartment.

The next day, I decided I really needed to get the mail. Another challenge was I needed to go up a couple of steps. A young man was coming down the street and saw me struggling and offered to help me, but I was too proud to accept it. I was determined to master walking with these things. I finally decided they must have been demon possessed or something as I would lean them up against the vanity in the bathroom to sit on the toilet, and as soon as I would get on the toilet, the crutches would come flying at me. I also decided they needed to send them to Iran as weapons of mass destruction.

They were having a women's conference, and one of my friends sponsored me to go with her. I met a wonderful woman there, and God placed me on her heart. She lived in close to the state line in a neighboring state, and we spent a lot of time on the internet with each other. She was such a blessing to me.

The time my broken ankle was healing was really hard as even though the church knew I wasn't to be driving, I was pretty much there on my own. My friend worked through the day, so she wasn't able to be much help to me. Even though some of the church people would drive right by my apartment on their way to church, I would have to call them before every service for anyone to pick me up. Before the ordeal was completely over, the assistant pastor and his wife had moved. There was a couple in the church who were also a real blessing to me, but I felt guilty having them help me. She was a double amputee, and he had really bad heart problems. They would come get me to take me to the store to get groceries. I would get what I needed, and he would load them in the car and then take them into the apartment.

At the end of the two weeks, I went back in to see the specialist to see how the ankle was doing. They took new X-rays and said it looked like it was healing slowly and to come back in another two weeks. I went back, and they said the X-rays were showing it was not healing at all. They apologized saying they had wanted it so badly that they thought they saw some healing before when there hadn't been. They started talking surgery. I told them, "I don't do surgeries."

They informed me it was looking like that was what they would have to do. I once again said, "You know that advertisement. 'I don't do windows.' Well, I don't do surgeries. I have reactions to medications, and I don't do surgeries." They decided they would wait a couple of weeks before making a decision.

Since I was able to get around a little better, I started looking for another job and was able to get it right away. Because of my working for the chamber of commerce, I was able to get my foot in the door. I was still on crutches and apologized to them but assured them it wouldn't affect my work.

The next time I went in to the doctor, they said they could see where it was healing, and they would go ahead and leave it in the boot. I was in that boot and on crutches for twelve weeks. When they took it off, since it hadn't been exercised nor had therapy, it was very stiff. I was determined to get it limbered up, so I started walking. My friends got after me for stressing it out from walking so far, trying to get it limbered up.

It was still pretty stiff when a friend invited me to go with her to a neighboring city to hear a special speaker. I was very excited to be out of the house and accepted. We were in the middle of the praise and worship when the speaker interrupted the service, saying God was telling him there was someone there who was having problems with their right ankle; and in the name of Jesus, it was healed. The praise and worship continued, and I started dancing with the music. When he got up to speak, he wanted to know who the ones were who had the problem with their right ankle. I raised my hand, and he told me to dance. That wasn't a problem as I had already been doing that. The next day, I went and helped with Bible school and was jumping around, playing the games with the kids.

I had worked for them for a couple of months when I sensed God was telling me I needed to empty the refrigerator of anything that was perishable. My brother's cancer was in advanced stages, and we knew it wouldn't be long. I was talking with my new friend from along the state line, and she said she was taking a trip to my home state. I asked what part, and she said the capital. I asked her if I could get the time off if I could go with her. My supervisor worked with me, so I could get the time off, and we headed back to my home state.

It was such an enjoyable trip and, for two people not really knowing each other very well, we knew it had been God who had put us together. We sang and prayed. When we would stop to eat, we would share a plate, and we would both be full. We both commented on how it was just God's doing as we were so compatible. She dropped me off at my son's, and he was going to take me to my eldest brother's the next day. The family all went to see *The Passion*, which was just being released, and then they took me to my brother's. We discussed the movie all the way up.

After we got there, my brother and my son had a really nice visit. (They had been at odds with each other from something that happened when Mom had been so sick.) Both of them commented later at how each had changed over the years, and my brother commented about how wonderful that son was. My sister-in-law and I had been after both of them to make amends as it happened at a time when there were a lot of stresses. We reminded them of all the years they had lost when they could have been enjoying each other just because they refused to forgive.

I spent the rest of the weekend at my brother's. We had some really good conversations, and I am so thankful for them. He had also got caught up in the Edgar Cayce philosophy of reincarnation. In one of our visits, he asked me about it. I told him that the Bible says, "Just as man is destined to die once and after that to face judgment" (Hebrews 9:27). He didn't say anything, but I knew he was facing the fact that he was dying.

On Monday, we made some of his favorite foods. His wife, his daughter-in-law, and I made homemade cabbage biscuits, which were one of his favorites. He had also asked that I make a homemade coconut cream pie. I tried to talk him out of the meringue, but he wanted one, so I made it. I have never had meringue on a meringue pie that turned out so perfectly, and I thanked God for helping me with it.

On Tuesday, my friend came by early, and we headed home. The return trip was just as good as the one coming out, and we spent time praying for my brother and his salvation.

On Wednesday, I went back to work. Usually, I wouldn't come home for lunch, but I felt I was supposed to that day. There was a message on the phone from my sister-in-law that said my brother had passed away that morning. She said he had fallen, and while he was lying there, he kept calling my name. My spirit man told me he wanted to tell me he had made it right with God. I still wanted confirmation and asked God to give me a sign.

I went back to work that afternoon and started making arrangements for returning to my birth state that weekend as his funeral was to be on Monday. He had also asked that my other brother and I play and sing for his funeral, so I started trying to get the songs he wanted. I worked until noon on Saturday and headed back to his place.

On that Friday, God gave me the confirmation I had asked for on my brother. My friend from the state line and I always met at the church during my lunch on Fridays to intercede and pray together. We were praying, and suddenly, God gave me this vision of my mother and my brother. They were looking down at me from heaven, and Mom was pointing her finger at me, shaking her hand, telling my brother, "This is what Beth does. This is what Beth does." He was always the one I confided in, but when it came to things of the spiritual nature, he never understood, so I would just jokingly tell him it was just his crazy sister thing. I burst out laughing, and my friend came running over, wondering if I was all right. I told her what I had seen, and we both laughed and felt it was the confirmation I had been asking for.

An aunt had passed away in California, and I felt like I also needed to go to her memorial service. When I was trying to make arrangements to go out, the family couldn't seem to come into agreement on when the memorial service would be, so I called the travel agency and asked God to give me the date I was to go. I scheduled the flight for the day I heard God say. Talk about God's timing—as always it was perfect.

I got to my cousin's house late at night on Saturday evening as my sister-in-law didn't think she would have room at her house. On Sunday morning, I went on over to my brother's house to wait for my other brother to come in so we could practice together. My sister-in-law decided she wanted me there with her, so my nephew went over to my cousin's to get my clothes while we practiced.

We had the funeral, and the next morning, I headed back home to literally change suitcases and head to the airport, an hour away, to fly out to California. I told God as I headed to the car with my bag that it would be so much easier on me if he would just transport me. I heard him say, "Get rid of your stuff, and I will." I told him I wasn't ready for that.

I spent the night with my former pastor and his wife, and they took me to the airport on Thursday to fly out to California. I had the privilege of getting to see my cousins and uncle whom I hadn't seen in years. My other brother had flown out, so we all had a wonderful visit. I was there for around four days when I flew to the state where my eldest son lived in to spend a few days with him before I came home.

I was sure glad there was nothing perishable in the refrigerator and that I had listened to God on getting it cleaned out. From the time I had gone out to see my brother for about six weeks, I was either gone or only home during the week.

While I was working at this place doing credit card collections, it was right next door to the church I attended. I asked about the possibility of going over during my lunch hour to pray and play the piano. They were very congenial and gave me the key. I had so many wonderful experiences with God during that time. I would usually go in and turn on the electric piano, never turning on the lights in the sanctuary. The sanctuary was totally enclosed, so it was completely dark when the lights weren't on. You could see a little crack of light between the doors, but that was all.

One day as I was playing, I could see this golden light over my shoulder. I would turn to see it, and it would move to the other shoulder. I knew it was God, and like with Moses, He was letting me see Him but was veiled. It was so awesome. I don't know how long it was there, but I found myself weeping as I played as God would come and visit me in such fashion. There were a number of other instances where I would feel His presence so strongly. Even though being there was hard in many ways, I can look back on those times and see how God was making me grow and teaching me in His ways. I am so thankful He cared so much about me that He chose to be near me in such a way.

I came back to work one afternoon that fall, and my former supervisor at the other place asked me if I had heard the news. I really hadn't been in much contact with the employees after I had left, so I told her no. She said one of them had called her saying they all left for lunch. They had come back to find a note on the door saying they had closed the business. I was so thankful I had listened to God and stepped out in faith in quitting that job. I was in the last crew hired at that place, and no one in the area was hiring. Once again, God had protected me.

I started having trouble with the coughing again. Early in the morning, I would have it when a certain woman came by who seemed to take a bath in perfume or was using some lotion that had a strong fragrance. It would pass after she left. Then they moved me up to the front of the building, and it really got bad. One time I was talking on the phone, and suddenly, I couldn't breathe. I was having trouble even talking. I hurriedly got off the phone, and the supervisor told me to go outside. I ran outside, fighting for my breath. When I came in, they asked what happened. I told them I didn't know as I didn't smell anything. The former supervisor was sitting next to me and asked if it was her lotion. It immediately sent me coughing again. She apologized as she hadn't realized it was the culprit.

The HR had called me in, said the coughing was bothering people, and wanted me to stop it. I told them what was triggering it off and asked if maybe they could do something about it. I was told it would be offensive to talk to someone about wearing so much perfume. I do have to admit I was bothered by it as they could do something about the perfume, but I couldn't do anything about the coughing, and it was okay for them to talk to me about something I had no control over.

The one friend who had sponsored me for the conference and I had become very close, and they would come over quite a bit for dinner as the college students had all moved away. They had a son who at first was so shy that he wouldn't eat in front of anyone. He got so comfortable being in my house that after the meal, he would eat the last broccoli from the serving bowl. She would get after him, and I would just tell her to let him do it as he was at Grandma's house and that told me he felt at home. The son and I had planned on going Christmas shopping together, but he decided he wanted to go with friends instead. I told him it was okay as we always had next year.

They moved back in the area, and one night I got a call from her saying she needed me to come to the hospital. Her son was dead. He hadn't come home that night when he was supposed to, which was very unusual for him. They kept looking for him and finally saw police lights a couple of country roads over. They decided to go over to where the lights were, and there was the pickup he had been driving. He always fastened his seat belt. We didn't know what happened, but he had been thrown from the vehicle and broke his neck.

I went to the hospital and sat by his body, praying for God to raise him back to life and commanding him to come back to life. I was doing it quietly as I was afraid someone might hear me and think I was crazy. I wish I would have been bolder, but I don't know if it would have made a difference. He did not come back to life, and we had funeral arrangements to make. He loved Elvis, so they played a lot of Elvis songs at his funeral.

To go to work, I had to cross the road they took him up to the hospital. There was no way I could get there from a different direction. Every time I would cross the road, I would burst into tears. It was very hard for me as it was just as though I had lost one of my own children. The parents had so much trouble dealing with it that they finally moved out of the area. I really missed them, but I could understand their decision.

My cousins, my brother, and I were all to inherit equally from my aunt and uncle's estate. When it was getting close for the estate to be dispersed, I started seeking God about what I was to do with it and what was ahead. I knew I would pay tithes on it as I always gave to God first as the Bible says to do. I felt he was telling me I was to get a fifth wheel to live in and was to get ready to move back to my home state.

My friend from a neighboring town and I started looking for a fifth wheel in the community where she lived as there were no distributors where I lived. The first search was Labor Day weekend, and none of the places were open, but they did leave some of the used carriages open for people to look at. I thought purchasing a used one would work, but God told me it was to be new. We also ran into some people who had owned a fifth wheel and gave us some pointers on what to look for. God had told me it was to be built in Canada. I knew nothing about fifth wheels, let alone ever thought of living in one.

The next weekend, I went up, and the dealerships were open, so we were able to look at the new ones and get more information. The next time I would go up, I would tell them what I wanted as far as breaks, tires, and such. It amazed them what I was learning about the fifth wheels and how quickly I was learning it. I give God all the glory as I had no idea what I was doing. The company I felt I was to deal with had told me that when I found what I wanted, they would find it for me.

I went back out to visit the kids for a week and, while I was there, looked at fifth wheels also. We came across one that I liked, and it was made in Canada. After further research, I found that the company that made them was considered to be a top-of-the-line manufacturer. I went back and told the dealership what I was wanting and gave them the model number. I also asked for a discount since I would be paying cash. They said they didn't give discounts as it was considered a recreational vehicle. I was going to be spending more money in just a couple of weeks than I had ever made and didn't want to be missing God's direction. I asked God to confirm if I was hearing Him right.

A couple of days later, I got a call saying the owner had decided that since I was paying cash, he would give me a 2 percent discount. I knew that was God confirming His direction once again. They searched but couldn't find the one I was wanting, so I really did end up with new as it was a special order. I wasn't going to get a fireplace, but something told me, since it was a special order, to go ahead and get it. (That turned out to be a great blessing.) Since it was a special order, it was going to take six weeks before I would have it.

They asked me if I had a truck to pull it, and I told them I didn't as I was waiting until I knew what size of truck I was going to need to pull the fifth wheel after I got it. They said they had a friend who had a car dealership and asked if they could have them look for a truck for me. I told them that would be great. It wasn't very long when I got a call wanting to know what I was doing that Saturday as they had my truck. I didn't have anything planned other than joining my friend for breakfast and prayer. We had our breakfast and went to check out the truck. They showed it to me, and it was the exact one God had shown me in a dream, so I knew it was to be mine. They offered to let me take it that day, but I told them I wanted to wait until I knew when I was going to have the money in hand. I did go ahead and traded before I had the money in hand, but I knew it was on the way. They gave me a good deal, and when I got back to my home state, I realized they had given me an even better deal than I thought.

I had taken the things I was going to put in the fifth wheel to the church until they contacted me saying the fifth wheel was ready for me to pick up. The pastor helped me get the truck loaded, so I could take the things the kids wanted back to them. I got the apartment all cleaned and started to crawl into the sleeping bag on the floor.

The craziest thought crossed my mind about a brown recluse being in the sleeping bag. I was really tired, so I shook the sleeping bag a little and crawled in to get some sleep before I pulled out in the morning. I woke up in the morning, and I noticed two small dots on my breast but just thought I had been bitten by a mosquito in the night. As I traveled across the state, I realized it was more than a mosquito bite. I had seen the progressions of a brown recluse bite from some pictures a friend had sent me on the internet, so I knew what to look for. One of the bites was on a scar I already had there. Within a couple of days, I had a huge sore, and it kept getting larger and getting discolored. I had tried putting things on it, and nothing was helping. I finally went to the doctor and was told it was a brown recluse bite and given some antibiotics for it. It cleared up quite a bit but still wasn't totally cleared up. I got a second dose, and it still hadn't totally cleared up. It was oozing some still when I received the call saying the fifth wheel was in.

I headed back, excited about getting my new home. I spent the night in a hotel and planned on picking the fifth wheel up the next morning. I went over to the dealership to pick it up to be told all the prep work had not been completed, and it would be another day. They offered to put me in the best hotel at their expense for the night until it was completed. I appreciated them for doing it for me. I found I had better amenities in the cheap hotel I stayed in than in the expensive one they put me in but was grateful for their kindness. While I was waiting, I purchased some of the things I was going to need for the fifth wheel.

The day was finally here for me to take possession of my new home. They went through the store and gave me a number of things like an outside rug and a step stool. Then they asked if I had ever pulled anything before. I told them I had only pulled a small trailer behind a car many years ago but nothing of this size. The owner said he would give me driving lessons if I would like, and I took him up on it. He drove it out to the loop and pulled over for me to take the wheel. We drove around the city, and he said I was driving like a pro but would be willing to make another trip around if I wanted. I told him if I was driving like a pro, I was out of here and took him back to the dealership.

I went to the church to get the things I had stored there and put them away. Then I headed back down the road toward home. Going down the road, I suddenly realized I was one of those vehicles I always hated meeting on narrow roads. I would also find myself sucking in my breath and holding it when I would go through construction areas where they had it buoyed off or when meeting another big rig on the road. I laughed as though sucking in my breath was going to make the rig and me smaller to get through. I made it back to my home state and was able to get it parked in the RV park I had reserved just west of the community God had told me to move to.

Chapter 11

The fifth wheel was really nice and just perfect for me. It was thirty-six feet long with four extensions. I had thought I would be claustrophobic in it, but I found that because of the way it was built, I had plenty of space. With just me in it, it didn't take a lot of cleaning, and I could have it done in less than an hour. I not only had the fireplace but I also had a built-in vacuum and a washer/dryer combination.

There was a tremendous learning curve when it came to taking care of it with all the tanks and everything, but I set out to learn what I needed to do. I had bought a pair of bib overalls for a fun church dinner we were doing, and those became a wonderful companion as I would climb under the fifth wheel to hook things up or to connect it to the truck. I never dreamed I would ever wear them again after that dinner, but I eventually wore them out, much to my dislike.

When I was pulling the rig, I would get all kinds of funny looks and comments. I would be told I wasn't dressed right to be pulling something like that. I would ask what I was supposed to look like and was informed I should have cowboy boots and Western wear. I just told them to talk to God as my body wouldn't fit in those types of clothes comfortably. I was also told I was too small to be pulling a rig of that size. I would just laugh at them and tell them my size didn't have anything to do with it as I was pulling it.

I loved the RV park/campground I was in, and they occasionally needed help during their busy season, so they would hire me to clean the bathroom and things like that. The neighbors were really pleasant to visit with, and it was like a close family. It was also fairly close to the church and town. I found that the truck didn't do very well on icy roads, but other than that, everything was good, and the trailer pulled great.

As I was pulling it across Wyoming, the winds were really bad. I did finally pull over and wait for the winds to calm down, but it wasn't because of the trailer. Meeting the eighteen-wheelers on the road, their trailers would be going all over the place from the wind gusts, and I was concerned they might be blown into my trailer.

I was going to the capital city quite a bit as my sister-in-law was not doing really well, and it was obvious she was really missing my brother. They had been married for forty-nine years when he passed away. They had done most everything together after he retired, so even though she had known he was dying, it left a real gap in her life. I was glad I didn't have to concentrate on working, so I could be with her as much as I was. We would go to the Red Hat Society together, and I would go with her to her grieving support group. Sometimes we would just sit and reminisce about my brother. She told her grief support group that I was the best when it came to helping someone grieving. I knew it was just God, and I gave Him all the glory.

The last day of February, after moving back to my home state, I received a call saying they had rushed my sister-in-law to the hospital due to a bleed out. She had struggled with heart problems for years, but when my brother was so sick, she had concentrated on making sure he had the care he needed. I was at a church event, so I immediately asked for prayer and planned to go up the next day. I called the next day, and she was doing fine and was being discharged.

The bleed outs continued for about two months. They were able to get her strong enough for open-heart surgery, but the projections were not favorable on her side. They said she had a 5 percent chance of making it off the operating table. She said she wanted to go ahead with the surgery, so they did it. She had always respected my relationship with God but had never wanted me to pray with her, and I always tried to honor that.

The night before surgery, she asked us all to gather around her bed with the doctor who was in the room and asked me to pray. We all prayed for a successful surgery and for the doctors and nurses. She said she had made it right with God, so if she didn't make it, she would be in heaven with my brother. The surgery went well, and she came through the surgery amazingly. We were all so encouraged at how well she was doing. I was staying at her place with my nephew, and we were driving to the hospital she was in, allowing us to be together.

That Sunday morning, we tried to call her to see how she was doing and if she needed anything before we left. We couldn't get an answer. We thought it was a little strange but thought maybe they had taken her for some tests or something. We got to the hospital to find they had sat her up for breakfast, and she bled out almost all her blood. There was no response. They put her on life support until they could run the tests to confirm if there was brain activity or not. My brother and she had set up directives on what to do in such a case, which made it a lot easier on the family. If either of them had to be on life support, it was not to be for more than seven days, and then we were to discontinue the life support.

The test came back; there was no brain activity, so that Tuesday morning, we gathered in her room to talk with the surgeon and make our decision. You could tell it was really hard for the surgeon to give us the news. We gathered in a circle, and my nephews asked me to pray. When we finished, we told the doctor how much we appreciated him and all he had done for her. Then the doctor asked if there was anything else he could do for the family before they took her off the life support. I looked at him and said there was one more thing he could do for me. He had a concerned look on his face, not knowing what to expect. I told him, "Smile. I have never seen you smile." And even though I knew his concern, I would really like to see him smile as I knew he had done all he could.

Then we had all the funeral arrangements and things to prepare for. I had told her I would be there for the boys to assist them in any way I could. We went directly from the hospital to the mortuary to start making the arrangements. And then I prepared to go pick up my second eldest son. I have to admit things are a little bit of a blur during this time about the time frame. I think I left the next morning to pick up my second eldest son in a neighboring state and returned home the same day. Then I went back to where my nephews lived for more funeral planning the next day. When I arrived home, my eldest son and his wife came that night really late. We visited until the early hours of the morning. I went back to where my nephews lived to practice with my other brother since we were to sing and play the piano and organ. We had the funeral shortly after we finished practicing.

Needless to say, when it was all over, I was exhausted, and I still had the flowers to take to the church and the rest of the cake to my daughters. I dropped the cake off to find they were having what they called a family reunion, but I don't remember being invited. I know I was pretty tired, but I'm sure I would have remembered something like that. They were just taking the burgers off the grill and thanked me for the cake. I don't remember my son-in-law asking me if I would like something. I headed home brokenhearted, knowing I still had to take my son back home the next day.

I fixed something to eat and visited with a cousin on my dad's side for a while who had come in and had to leave the next day. It was getting late, so I called to see when they were going to bring my second eldest son home, only to be informed by my son-in-law that I could pack his things and pick him up on my way to take him home. I tried reasoning with him in that I would also like to spend some time with him since I hadn't been able to, and he just kept trying to yell over me, which was his way of doing things. Then he hung up on me. I will admit by this point I was mad. I called back, and he would not pick up the phone. In the course of the conversations, he said if it wasn't for me, my children wouldn't have any problems, and they all felt that way. I left a message that I loved my daughter, but I did not like him. They did finally bring him home, but then they sat outside and talked for a long time.

The next morning, I proceeded to start back to take my son home. I was so physically tired and emotionally exhausted from all that I had been through. On the way back, I stopped at a hotel and spent the night as I knew I was no longer in any condition to drive. My youngest son called, and I didn't even pick up the phone. Later, I did call him back, telling him that at the time I just couldn't talk, and burst out crying. He informed me he didn't feel that way, and he had already left when that all transpired.

It took me a long time to forgive my son-in-law for all the pain he caused during a very painful time. I had learned that when it is hard to forgive, ask God to help you forgive until you know you have forgiven them. I knew I had been able to forgive when I knew he wanted tickets to something I was helping with and had extra tickets. I gave them to him and didn't even feel resentment toward him. Later, he had an accident and totaled his vehicle. My first response was "Is he okay?" I knew God had helped me forgive. In my opinion, he is still a jerk, but I don't hate him or wish him any harm.

Then my eldest son decided he was moving back to his birth state. The first time, he brought the children and left them with me, waiting on the house to sell so they could follow. The house didn't sell, so his wife came to get them that Christmas. While I had them, I was doing property management for a friend as it worked really well for getting the children back and forth to the charter school they were attending.

After they took the children back with them, I started doing home health care. The next spring after school was out, my son came back with the children and stayed with me until his wife could join them. I was still in the RV park and suddenly received a notice they wanted us out in three days. They said my grandson had done some things and that he was a problem. I found out later that it was actually one of the tenant's daughters and her cousin, and they were blaming the things on him. I'm not saying he never did anything, but I thought it was a little strange as my neighbor had become like a grandfather to him, and they were always going places and doing things together.

A friend said the trailer park she lived in had just said they were opening up for RVs, so I contacted them. They rented to me, and later, the county said I couldn't be there, but the manager fought for me. They finally did give her favor, letting me stay, and I praise God for His favor and for the manager that she was willing to fight for me.

That July 4, we were all at my second youngest son's, celebrating. Of course, the traffic was terrible; and the next morning, I had a home health care job in the mountains. I didn't have a signal, so as soon as I got down where there was a signal, I checked to see if there were any messages. There was one from my son, and he very seldom called, so I knew something was wrong, and I needed to check the message immediately. As soon as I heard his voice, he started breaking up, and I could hear the pain in his voice. He said, "Mom, my ex-wife had an accident. I know we had our problems, but she didn't deserve this." I immediately assumed it was because of the traffic the night before.

When I was able to contact him, I found she had a trampoline accident and had broken her neck. Because traffic that time of night after the fireworks was always a gridlock, it had taken the ambulance longer to get there than usual. They were figuring she had been at least eighteen minutes without oxygen.

Since her mother lived in a foreign country, when she needed someone to talk to, she would many times call me. She had become a lot like a daughter even though she and my son were divorced. I immediately went to the hospital to be with her and had decided I would not be leaving until her mother was able to be there with her. I felt my son was handling it with wisdom above his years, especially when it came to the girls. They told us they didn't think she would make it, and if she did, it was going to be a long recuperation period. I was praying hard as I knew God could totally restore her, and the girls were praying for her restoration also. I did make sure to pray the Sinner's Prayer over her as I knew she hadn't been living for the Lord and that the hearing is the last to go. I wanted to make sure that no matter what happened, she would be going to heaven.

Her mother came and announced she didn't come for any funeral and that she believed for her daughter's complete healing. I told her I was agreeing with her. The next day, she said she had a dream of her daughter in heaven, and she was so happy that she wanted us to let her go. I do have to admit I was a little upset as I am not one who likes changing horses in the middle of the stream, but I had to honor her decision.

They made the decision to pull life support. My son refused to be a part of that decision-making as he did not want the girls to think he had killed their mom, but he did stipulate that she remain on life support until after the eldest girl's birthday. He didn't want to have her mother passing on her birthday. The decision had been made that after midnight, they would take her down and remove the life support. I offered to be there with her mother just for support. Her mother accepted, and we were there together as she breathed her last breath. Within five minutes after removing life support, she passed on. There were some questions about her death, and I do pray that someday we will find out the truth about what actually happened. There were so many things that happened the night of the accident that were out of her character. I was so glad my eldest son was there for me through all this.

We had just worked through all that turmoil, and I just arrived on a job. As I walked in the door to the job, I got a call from my youngest son saying the ambulance was rushing his son to the hospital. His son had stopped breathing. I told the lady I was out of there and headed to the hospital. She understood, which I was very grateful for. I arrived at the hospital, and he still was not breathing on his own. I started calling in the prayer warriors as I knew we had a serious situation. Since they couldn't get him to breathe on his own, they decided to fly him to the children's hospital.

I contacted the children. I look back in amazement of how God orchestrated the whole thing. The other grandmother had been watching our two grandsons, and one came in saying the baby had quit breathing. She immediately went in, realized he wasn't breathing, and called the ambulance. The ambulance was close to their house but many times was out on calls. This time, it wasn't out. They came right away. I had just arrived at my job when I got the call. Any later, I wouldn't have answered the phone until the job was completed.

When they decided to fly him out, my second youngest had just left work; and since he worked close to where they were taking my grandson, he was there before the ambulance arrived. My son's fiancée had an uncle who was a minister who had just flown in on his way home, and he went immediately to the hospital. I can't say I remember exactly what I did other than I had some of the grandchildren in the truck with me, and one mentioned everyone should drive a truck like that because they could see so well. Anyway, we all got to the hospital within a short time of each other.

When my grandson arrived, they still didn't have him breathing on his own. The girls who had lost their mother were very distraught and justifiably so. The children's hospital had a sign stating that no children were allowed in the rooms, and the children were so terrified that they were going to lose their cousin. Finally, I went to the head nurse and told her the situation. I said, "I don't usually ask people to make exceptions for me, but these children just lost their aunt/mother in an accident, and they need confirmation their cousin is going to be okay." She said she would allow them to go in for just a few minutes. We prepared them on what to expect so it wouldn't be so traumatic to them and took them in.

He did start breathing on his own, and I praise God for the miracle God worked on him. Some could say that God should have prevented it, and I know He could have, but I am also thankful for the many things that worked together. Only God could have synchronized that so well.

While I was caring for this lady, I went to get cat food for her at the pet store. As I was going in, this woman came out with the cutest dog. It was so friendly, and I just fell in love with it. I asked her what the breed was, and she said a papillon. I had never heard of that breed, but I said that one day I would have one. I went on about my work and didn't think about it anymore.

One day I received a call from one of my sons asking if I wanted a dog. I told him I really didn't want one but asked why he was asking. He said a friend had been taking care of a dog and couldn't do it anymore, but the owner couldn't take her. As a result, they were going to put her down. I told them I would take her.

I had her for about a year, and the original owner decided they wanted her back. Since she had children, I was feeling bad. I took the dog to her apartment to see if the dog would still remember them. As I was getting ready to go and take the dog back, she decided to let the boy take her out to go to the bathroom. The boy never came back, and I waited for quite a while. Finally, I decided I would go and contact her the next day to see how the dog had done; and if the dog didn't do well, I would come get her. The next day when I called, she said the dog was doing great and for me not to come get her.

My kids had fits as the grandchildren had always enjoyed the dog, and it was wrong of me to put the other kids above the grandchildren. I decided to see what I could do to find a replacement. I called a friend who used to work at the humane center. He said he no longer worked there, but he had gotten some dogs on Craigslist and told me to check there. I went on Craigslist, and the first dog that came up was a papillon. I contacted the number and left a message. I didn't hear anything, so I decided evidently that I was not to have it. I went online again, and it was still there, but I still hadn't heard anything. Finally, I felt like I just had to wait.

About a week later, I received a call from the owners. They said after they had listed him, they were told that when purebred dogs were listed, if there was not a rehoming fee, people would use them in the mills. As a result, they were going to charge a rehoming fee. The people who were ahead of me either didn't want to pay the fee or had gone a different direction, and now they had come to me. The rehoming fee they were asking was $100. I didn't know where I was going to get the $100, but something told me to go ahead. I have always had problems paying out money for an animal when there are children going hungry, but I went ahead.

We set up the appointment, and I had made plans to get some dog food and toys for him. I was running late and was concerned about it when I got a call from the owner. She apologized as she was running late also. I explained why I was running late, and she was surprised. When I opened the door, she said she was dropping the rehoming fee to $50. The dog totally made himself at home. We visited for a while when she said she needed to leave. I told her I needed to get my wallet so I could pay her. She said she had decided to drop it to $25. I got my wallet and started to pull out my checkbook when she informed me that there would be no charge; he was mine.

When my son came home, the dog went over and jumped on my son's lap and started licking his face. That had been one of our concerns as the dog had been abused by a previous owner and had a problem with men. God had given me my papillon, and it was at a time when I really needed encouragement. God heard me say I had wanted a papillon; He remembered and gave me one at the perfect time.

After that, things actually settled down a little bit for quite a while. My son's wife did come and was in the area for a while but then decided she wasn't staying, so she took the children and went back. He did follow her shortly after that.

One morning I went out the door of the fifth wheel to find parts of an animal laid in a specific order on the step. I immediately knew it was something that had to do with witchcraft or Satanism. I had been doing some research concerning the days of sacrifices and holidays in the Satanic religion, wanting to know the correlation between crazy things happening and their holidays. I asked God who had done it as I wasn't aware of anyone involved in Satanism, so how would any of them know where I lived? God told me that Satan knew where I lived. I thought, *How nice.*

Later, I was doing some yard work and looked under the skirting. There was a large butcher knife hidden behind the skirting. Also, many times, I would wake up feeling like I had been in a fight and would have bruises on my body. I would ask God what was going on, and He would tell me I was fighting demons all night. Many years before, I had told God I wanted to be like Paul and pray in the spirit more than anyone else, and the grandchildren would say I prayed in the spirit all night. I don't know why I didn't wake up, but I know it was the praying in the spirit that saved me.

I continued working home health care and started taking care of a woman in her early nineties. I took care of her for a number of years. At first, it was just a couple of hours a day, and then it went to full time plus. She was the first person under the care of hospice whom they had ever graduated off their care. She was quite an amazing lady, and many of us who cared for her are still in contact. She was a retired lieutenant colonel's wife in the Air Force. Some who struggled with her referred to her as a Hitler, but as long as you made sure she had her coffee when she woke up, you didn't usually have a problem with her.

I had been taking care of a Jewish woman who was a Holocaust survivor when my ninety-plus-year-old client got so sick that she needed twenty-four-hour care. When I first started taking care of the Holocaust survivor, she told me to leave because Christians hated Jews. I told her I would gladly leave if she wanted me to, but I couldn't leave until they could get someone to come in and replace me. She didn't like that but finally decided I could stay. I told her if they claimed to be a Christian and hated Jews, then they were not a good Christian as Jesus, whom they served, was a Jew.

When they pulled me off her to take care of my other client needing twenty-four-hour care, she was very unhappy. I tried to make it better by telling her the other client didn't have any family here to help with her care, and that was why they were putting me with her full time. It was the truth, but she informed me she didn't have anyone around either (which she did) and that she needed her Bet (which was what she called me). It made me feel good that God had helped me help her understand my love for her and that she now didn't want me to leave.

I took care of the ninety-plus-year-old client until her death at the age of ninety-seven. When I first started taking care of her, she considered prayer a private thing, and she would ask that I pray for her but would never let me pray out loud for her. I grew very close to the family and was in contact with her son quite a lot about her care. The nurse who also came in said I was the best she had seen in the field.

My client loved to cook, and one time a friend had taken me out to eat at an Italian place. We ordered the Italian chili they had on the menu. I had never tasted it before, so I wanted to try it. I literally made a pig of myself trying to find out what was in it, and when we left, I was pretty sure I could make it. I was telling her about it, and she asked, "Do you think you know what is in it?" I told her I thought I did.

She said, "I'll buy the ingredients if you'll make it." So we made Italian chili together.

Another time, she was commenting on how terrible she felt because she couldn't cook anymore. I asked her what made her think that way. She commented, "Because you girls are here to do it." The girls may have regretted me telling her, but I told her we were there to help her and that if she wanted to cook, we were supposed to help her. That really delighted her, and from then on, if she felt up to it, she was in the kitchen helping where she could.

One time my client said she had a dream, and she knew it was telling her that she would be passing soon. She commented that she was so afraid and didn't want to die alone. I told her I would do everything in my power to make sure I was there when she passed. She asked me to pray for her out loud. I was going out with a friend to eat when I received a call from the caregiver for that shift saying they were on the way to the hospital with her. She had a stroke, and it was serious. I asked the friend to take me to my car as I needed to go to the hospital. I stayed with her until her son could get there.

When he arrived, I told him I knew they didn't need me anymore, but I had promised her I would stay with her, so I would go off the clock so he would not be charged for my being with her. He wanted to know the number of the company. He called them and told them they wanted me to continue getting paid until she passed away. I was with her as I had promised when she passed away. I thanked God once again for His favor that I was to be paid during that time when I had planned on it just being a donation.

After she passed away, the company I had been doing home health care through said they didn't have any jobs for me. I don't know what was going on as I had people saying they had requested me, and they had been told I was too busy. After my client died, I was really exhausted, so I spent some time trying to get some rest. I had not only been taking care of her better than one hundred hours a week but I was also giving piano lessons to my grandchildren and some other underprivileged children.

I had been a number of months with just small jobs and was getting behind on everything. They had my client's memorial service, and as I was leaving, her son asked if he could walk me to the truck. I found myself thinking that was a little strange as we had a good enough friendship that I thought he should have felt comfortable just going with me. We were talking, and when we got almost to the truck, he handed me an envelope and said he and his mother wanted me to have that for the excellent care I had given her. In the envelope was enough money for me to get my bills paid. I thanked God once again for His goodness.

I had also applied and been accepted for my ordination with Morris Cerullo World Evangelism. To get the ordination papers after taking all the classes and tests, you had to attend a conference. I had committed to going to the conference before my client had died and then was wondering how I would be able to go as

I didn't feel comfortable going if I didn't have money to pay my bills. God had resolved that problem, but now I had the problem of getting to Chicago to get my credentials.

I was telling this to my friend whom I had shopped for the fifth wheel with, and she said she had some flight miles but needed to check with her husband about giving them to me. She didn't know if she had enough, but she would check. Her husband gave his consent if there were enough without having to purchase some. The first time she looked, she was short. When it came time to get the tickets, she looked again, and there was enough. She was totally surprised as she hadn't used her card. She called with me on the phone to make sure, and they confirmed that was right. She purchased the tickets with the miles she had acquired from use of her credit card.

I hadn't reserved a hotel room as they will let you get them with someone else after you get there. God gave me a really wonderful roommate, and we had such a good time together. The only meals I had were the ones provided with the conference. The conference was so powerful that I think I could have flown home without the aircraft.

I was so excited about the ordination. I had applied once before and had been rejected as two of the three people I had used for references said they hadn't known me for more than two years. I was really hurt as I had known one when I had been the office manager of that church, and he was a deacon. The other I had known for many years as every time I would come back, I would seek his counsel. This time when I registered, the woman at the table told me to stay there as the director of ordination wanted to talk with me. My first thought was *What's happening now?* When she got there, she said she just had to meet me. They had never had anyone apply for ordination who had come with such high recommendations and such a high standard of living for Christ. I was so surprised.

When I received the CD of my ordination, I was so surprised. I was just lost in the presence of God, and I could hear Papa Cerullo coming closer. I wasn't paying so much attention, so when he stood in front of me, he said "wow" three times. I did write and ask what he saw, but I have never received an answer.

I got back and was able to get a job with the company taking care of an elderly man in a neighboring town. He and his family were delightful to work with, and they were all so close. It was really great working for such an awesome family. He always loved doves, and each morning there would be a row of doves sitting on the electric lines behind the house. He would watch them while we ate breakfast and talk about them. After he passed away, some of his family wanted me to take care of some of the other family members; but because of the contract I had signed to not have any of my own clients, I had refused, telling them they would need to talk with the company I was working with.

Then I started taking care of a woman who was moving into her daughter's house. They needed to do some remodeling, so they had put her in a care facility where I would go and stay with her. When the remodeling was done, I would take care of her at the house. The daughter decided she didn't like the way my employer was doing, so she took the classes so she could open her own business to care for the elderly. She offered me a private contract job through her company for more money, and I took advantage of the offer. Everything was going well when they realized she was starting to go downhill, and they felt the need to start looking for a care center to put her in. They wanted to get her in while she still had money enough to get her in one of the better ones. The room suddenly became available, leaving me once again without a job.

During that time, I was also informed that my stepson whom I had gotten close to had been diagnosed with stomach cancer. We had been working together on some plans we thought might help both of us with finances. With that, our plans fell by the wayside. It was my idea, but he had the knowledge to be able to make it happen. It broke my heart as we had become pretty close.

After the family put my client in the care center, I kept looking for jobs and couldn't find one. I would put in applications and be told I didn't have the qualifications. I couldn't figure out what was going on as nurses told me I was the best they had seen. Finally, I applied for unemployment. I was refused because one employer said I had stolen from them. I couldn't figure out how they could say something like that. Finally, the unemployment office said I was stealing their client. They were saying I had stolen that client when actually I had changed employers. I thought about fighting them on it but decided against it. I don't know if it was the right decision or not. God only knows.

I finally ended up losing everything and declaring bankruptcy. I really struggled with it as I had always paid my tithes and offerings and trusted that God would provide as He said in His Word. I was heartbroken and couldn't understand why. I felt like God had forgotten me and deserted me. I had a problem with trying to trust Him to provide for me for a long time after that. I am so glad God is patient and understanding through those times.

I had found a place where I could rent a room, and I would share the house with someone. The person talked like we had a lot in common. I got moved in, and within a couple of weeks, I realized we didn't have as much in common as he had led me to believe. It was in a trailer, and the manager of the trailer park said I couldn't stay there as I didn't have a job. I had enough coming in from my social security that I knew I would be able to pay my rent, but the manager wouldn't reconsider. I was walking and praying, asking God what I should do and what His plan was for me.

About that time, the phone rang, and it was my second youngest son asking how things were going. I said I needed to look for something else and told him what was happening. He said that was the reason he was calling. He was wondering if I would stay with the children through the summer and help out as one of the daughters who lost her mother was really giving them problems. I told him I would and made arrangements to move in.

Mother's Day was shortly after I moved in, and I had been invited to a tea for mothers the day before. While I was there, they gave us a bouquet of flowers. I asked my son if it would be okay to take the girls up to the cemetery and put the flowers on their mother's grave. He gave his consent, so we went up and cleaned around the tombstone as we talked and cried together. I felt it was very helpful to them to have that time to grieve over the loss of their mother.

Later, I was able to talk some with the one who was giving them the problems. I was able to tell her that even though I hated losing everything like I had, to be there with her and to help her through this time was worth far more than everything I lost, and I would gladly lose it all as I felt she was more valuable than that. I knew her father would not have asked me if I hadn't lost everything, so there wasn't anything to keep me from coming to help with her.

When the summer was over, they asked me to find a place of my own. I was looking for something and was told they would let me know after the holiday, but I was feeling like I needed to get out and grabbed the first thing available. I rented a furnished basement where we shared the kitchen and the laundry room. It wasn't the best, but it worked. After the weekend, I received a call that I had been accepted for the other place. I should have called and cancelled on the basement, but I didn't want to cause an imposition on the landlady.

Since I no longer needed the truck, my son was able to work with one of his neighbors who worked at a car dealership for trading. I was able to get a Saturn and money back, which I was thankful for. The bankruptcy lawyer also said that he was sure I was being blackballed by my previous employer, but we had no way of proving it. I knew I had to forgive them and turn it over to God.

I was able to find a job in a neighboring town, and I felt things were finally turning around. In a lot of ways, they were, and it was a great relief.

Chapter 12

I worked the job for quite a while. It is always so amazing how God puts you in the right place at the right time. I was at the age they were requiring me to go on Medicare. I was being told I was going to have to find a medical provider and all the things they were requiring me to jump through. I had pretty much decided I wasn't going to take out the insurance they were requiring if I went on Medicare. The place I was working was taking the new enrollments for Medicare. Had I not been working there, my decision would have cost me a lot of money in the end. It was very overwhelming trying to find a medical doctor as my doctor was Dr. God, and they wouldn't accept that as my medical provider.

I sat and cried with all I had gone through, and trying to make the decisions for Medicare was so overwhelming. I also thought of my mother and was so thankful she had my eldest brother to help her through a lot of that. I knew how overwhelming it was for me, and I had taken some college classes on insurance and had an idea of some of what I was dealing with. I also thought of the many others who had to deal with it all and how overwhelming it must have been to them.

I did the open enrollment period and then took more training so I could work on the side where we processed the renewal of prescriptions. I worked with many wonderful people, but the job was frustrating. There were many databases that we had to use, but we only had password to about half of them. As a result, we always had to ask a supervisor to get us in. Also, they were changing the way to do things daily but neglected to get the information down the chain of command. As a result, so much of the time, we were working without having all the information we needed. I became very frustrated as I could not give the type of customer service I liked to give.

One day I was working, and my supervisor came up. As soon as I finished my call, she logged me out and told me to come with her. I told her my shift wasn't over yet, and she told me she was aware, but she needed to talk with me. I followed her back to the area, and she said the contracting company had said she had to fire me. I asked what I had done wrong. She said nothing, but the main company was saying I had referred someone to file a complaint with Medicare when we had been instructed not to. I told her I had taken a complaint, but I made sure it was taken from the person themselves and not a relative like we had been trained to do. The daughter had asked if they could file a complaint with Medicare, and I told her she could, which was the truth, but I had not told her she could until she asked. My supervisor said every one of the trainers and quality people had listened to the call, which was perfect in every way. The company was refusing to fire me but had to figure out what they were going to do with me.

I got to spend the rest of the day watching her work. They told me to take the next day off with pay, so I did. I had accepted an invitation to go on a mission trip to Las Vegas and also to Kenya, so I worked on the letters for the mission trips at home and got paid for it. I had to love God's sense of humor. The following day, I went in and had taken the letters to finish during my lunch and breaks. I got there, and nobody had any idea what they were going to do with me yet, so they told me to find something to do while they figured out what to do with me. Once again, I was getting paid to work on the fundraising letters. By the time they decided what to do with me, I had the letters completed.

The new department was really easy to pick up, and I always had weekends off. The supervisor was a little bit of a challenge. One day he was getting on my case and being very disrespectful to me. Since we were about the same age and I knew the culture he came from, I made the comment that he should treat his elders more respectfully. He came back saying I wasn't his elder and asked what year I was born. I told him, and he never treated me that way again.

They had already told me I could have the time off for the mission trips, and he informed me he wasn't going to let me have it. I don't know exactly what I did, but he ended up giving me the time off I had requested. I knew in my heart I was supposed to go on both trips even though it was a real step of faith.

The landlady of the basement I had been living in decided she was getting married to her ex-husband and had given me instruction not to speak to him as he didn't like talking to strangers. I came in one day, and he spoke to me, and I responded. She wasn't very happy about that. Then she informed me she wanted me to take care of their animals while she was on their honeymoon. It was during the time I was to be gone on one of the mission trips, so she informed me she wanted me to move out.

A couple at my church decided they would let me stay with them for free as their way of helping me financially with the mission trips. I did try to give them some money to help while I was there. The money from the Las Vegas trip had come in, and I was able to go on that trip. I was really struggling in trying to get the money for the trip to Kenya. I had missed the deadline for the first deposit, and they called asking me what to do. I strongly felt God telling me to send out one last set of letters and see what happened.

One morning I was at the table, and a call came in asking if I was sitting down. I told them I was. They told me the rest of the money I needed for the trip had come in, plus overflow. I was so excited. The people I was staying with felt I should ask for the overflow back since I needed to find a place after I returned home. I have always felt that if I give to God, I don't ask for it back. They were not really happy about it. There had been a young lady who also needed funds, and with the overflow, she had the funds, so she could go.

Before we left, we gathered together in a circle and sang the old hymn "I'll Go Where You Want Me to Go." As we sang it, the tears started rolling down my cheeks. I stood at an altar when I was a child singing that song. After all these years, I was seeing that commitment manifested.

Once again, the tears started rolling as soon as I set foot on Kenyan soil. Growing up, I had always told my mother I felt like a huge black singer on a stage, singing. Mom never brought us up concerned about skin color, but she would say, "Elizabeth, you know you're white."

I would say, "I couldn't help it. That is how I saw myself." It was like I was home; I was finally home. Also, growing up, when the music would come on, I always wanted to dance. I was truly finally home. They nicknamed me the white black woman, and I immediately fell in love with the people.

This was my first international ministry, and we saw God do some wonderful things. I saw one man's leg grow out. I prayed with another mother and child who had AIDS to the point that they had oozing sores. We saw God heal them and totally restore them to health. I found God using me to prophesy over Kenya of His desire for them to have revival, and He wanted to use Kenya to take the gospel to the world.

God also reminded me how my mother had always wanted to work in an orphanage in Africa. Many of the people whom I was ministering to would have been orphans when she would have been here if God opened up the door so she could come. I was so humbled to think God would allow me the honor of ministering to the people she had desired to help. One young native man who had joined the team was an orphan. We did take an offering to help him get his dowry. As he was getting ready to get on the bus to prepare the last part of the wedding, I told him he was no longer an orphan as I would be honored to be his mama. He was thankful that I wanted him for my son.

One day most of the team decided they were going on a safari on their day off, but there were a couple of us who decided to go with our leader to a meeting. This special meeting had been arranged, and there were better than one hundred pastors from different denominations at the meeting. Our leader was going to speak, and we were anticipating great things. We were praying all the way for God to minister to them and use us to bring unity between them.

We really felt the opposition from the enemy as we went to the meeting. We got there without any problems. We went to unload our leader, who is a paraplegic, with a motorized wheelchair, and the hoist would not go down. We worked and worked and couldn't get it to go down. Finally, they asked some people to move their cars so they could back up to the building we were to minister in. They backed the van as closely as they could to the building, but there was still about a six-inch gap from the van lift to the top step. We prayed and watched the driver and one of our team members pick up that wheelchair and carry it to the building so the wheelchair could roll in the rest of the way. Those wheelchairs are heavy, and our leader is a tall man, so we knew it was God. Our leader ministered for four hours, and when we were done, we saw all the ministers join hands and kneel, vowing to unite for the kingdom of God.

I found myself ministering on what seemed like the strangest things just to find it was the very thing the people were struggling with. One message was about the importance of a name and how the name can be a curse or a blessing. The Bible talks about that, and at the end, we asked people who had been given a name that was a curse to come forward for prayer. There were so many of them wanting the curses of their names changed, and we would proclaim a blessed name. There were many who were having other health issues because their families had dedicated them to demons or placed curses on them that they could never eat certain foods. We came against the the curses, and the next day, the testimonies were plentiful. Depressions were broken; people were able to eat food or meat that they had never been able to eat before.

This was also training for me as I always had to have everything so organized. We had a team of eleven people, and then we had a number of native pastors who joined us. Also, since this was the first mission trip of this type and the first international mission trip, there were a lot of learning curves. We would be told to pack our suitcases to go to a certain place and that we would be there for a certain length of time. I would find I had packed part of the things I needed to take with me but left a lot at the hotel that was our central base. I would end up not having my towel or something else that was needed, so I would just improvise to make things work.

Just before we were to leave, we were notified that our tickets had been cancelled, so they were trying frantically to get us tickets to get back home. Coming over, some of the team had their flight changed, and that was what was causing the problems with our return flight. To add to the confusion, the airport had a fire, so they had to do a lot of their things manually, and everything was pretty much makeshift to try to keep things going. We did arrive home without any problems once we were able to get on our return flight.

I arrived back from Kenya and started looking for a place to live. With what I made, it was going to be close if I found anything, but I kept looking. I had my dog, and the problem I was running into was trying to find a place that would allow me to have him. A person was also willing to share a place with me, but two-bedroom apartments were too much for us to afford also. I had applied for government-assisted apartments, and they said I made $50 too much to get in. My kids laughed at me as I said I really didn't want to live there anyway as it had old people living there. They informed me I was old and laughed. I told them I knew, but these people were shuffling their feet and pushing walkers, and I wanted to stay full of vitality.

I came home one day, and they told me they wanted me to leave and gave me a certain time to be out. The prices of apartments had gone sky high as there had been a flood taking out many people's homes, so the demand was high. With the demand, it threw me totally out of the market. I finally decided I would find someone to take the dog, and I would go to the homeless shelter until I could find something. I called some of the children to see if they would take the dog. My daughter asked what I was going to do, and I told her. She informed me I wasn't going to a homeless shelter but that I could sleep on her couch, and the dog could stay with me. I stayed there with her for about six months.

I put in an application at an apartment complex. They told me they didn't have any openings at the time, but I paid for the credit check, and they had just opened up to allowing pets. I had a peace that God was providing that apartment for me.

I had received word from my brother that his granddaughter had passed away and that they had also lost the baby she was carrying. I had received word just a couple of days before that he had also lost another great-grandbaby. I really felt I needed to be with him through this time of great loss. He lived quite a distance, so I had made plans to get an early start. Things kept happening that were causing delays, and I was getting very frustrated. I was finally able to breathe a sigh of relief as I was on my way.

I was headed up the hill just outside of town when I saw police lights come on. I tend to have a heavy foot, so I was almost positive why I was being stopped. I pulled over, and he asked if I knew how fast I was going. I was honest and told him I had no idea as I was trying to get out of town to get to my brother's due to the deaths. I thought I was holding up really well, but when I said that, the tears just started flowing. I really don't believe I was going as much over as I later checked the speed limit in that area, and I would have been flying low if I had been. I had always been taught to honor them, and I was definitely in no mood to argue with him and cause problems and more delays. He checked all my information and gave me the ticket. Before he moved on, he said, "Fasten your seatbelt, slow down, and set your cruise control, ma'am. Your family doesn't need another death to deal with."

As I went down the road, I was fuming to myself mostly that I wasn't watching the speedometer more closely or set the cruise control. I did set the cruise control, and when I got about three-fourths of the way, there was a sign over the road stating there had been an accident ahead and to be prepared for slower traffic. It seemed like I had driven a long time before I finally came on the accident. An eighteen-wheeler heading west had lost control and rolled over into the eastbound traffic. The trailer covered the whole left lane. They had the trailer about half-unloaded. It suddenly hit me, and I began to thank God with tears in my eyes. Had God not stopped me by the police officer, I would have been in that spot when the trailer tipped, and I would have probably been in that lane. I had to thank the officer for not only doing his job but also saving my life.

That wasn't the first time God had delayed me on trips and prevented me from being involved in an accident. I have wondered over the years how many times we have gotten upset about the delays when it had been orchestrated by God as a means of protecting us from the unseen. God is so good and so wonderful to those who love and serve Him. We can never thank Him enough for what He does.

I had found a new job that was closer and a lot easier company to work for. I was relieved not to have to drive so far. I hadn't been working there for very long when I got a call saying an apartment had suddenly opened up, and I could move in within the week. It was in the same community as my new job. My daughter was planning on moving also and was concerned I wasn't going to have a place. God once again came through just in the nick of time. I was able to get moved in, and my daughter moved at the end of the month.

Chapter 13

From here on, I am going to change the format a little. Rather than specify each trip, I will mostly tell of the many things God did and the testimonies of God's help, guidance, and protection through it all.

I strongly felt God wanted me to go to Uganda and back to Kenya. God miraculously opened the doors for me to go. This trip was quite a walk of faith. Before I left, a friend and his wife prophesied over me. The prophecy was really different from the ones I had ever received before. He said things weren't going to go the way I had thought, but I should not be concerned as God was in control, and He was taking care of me. There would be curses spoken over me, but they would not be able to come to fruition as God was taking care of me.

I had sent out letters for fundraising, and finally, the money for the tickets came in the night before but nothing more. I called, and the very flight I had been looking at had one seat available, which I grabbed. I called my friend to see if she could take me to the airport. She said God had told her to fill her car with gas and be ready to go somewhere. The car was filled, and she just needed to take a shower. She got there, and we immediately left.

We arrived at the airport at the time I needed to be there for check-in. I had wondered what I was going to do for the visa as I didn't have the money for it. My friend said that God told her to give me all the money in her purse. It was exactly the amount I needed for the visa. I had a pastor from Kenya who was to join me but couldn't until after I had been there for four days. While I was in flight over there, the people we were working with had sent me an email saying not to trust all people from Uganda as some were just after your money. That wasn't a problem as I didn't have any, but I didn't get the letter until I had been there a week and a half as I didn't have internet access.

I went through customs, and they told me they would not accept my money as it wasn't crisp enough. I didn't know what to do, so I started asking questions. The security was not very helpful, but God finally did bring someone who helped me. I asked the security if it was okay to leave my bag there while I went around to the exchange to see if they could exchange some crisp dollars for the ones I had. They told me I had to put my bags in a little room, which I did. The exchange people were really nice and exchanged the money for me. I had found myself almost in tears because the security was so rude.

Then I had tried to find my hosts as I had never seen them before. I was able to find them, and they started looking for a place to get food. I was thinking they seemed to be unorganized for someone who was expecting me, but I didn't really think a lot about it. They got some food, and we went to their place and had something to eat. The next day was a Saturday, and I had been told I would be speaking on TV. They said they were going to get their hair done and would be back to take me for the TV program. They never showed up. When they came back, they said they had decided to cancel the TV interview.

Their orphanage was right close, and there was a little girl who they said had been found by the police, and they had given her the name of Triza 2 as they already had a Triza in the orphanage. She looked like she was probably around four years old. She didn't talk, but she would sit on my lap. I would hold her and pray over her every chance I got. When I left, she would count for me and sing while I held her. She was so sweet. I wanted to bring her home with me, but I knew I couldn't.

The Sunday after church, the pastor asked me for money for gas to get to the open-air meetings he had scheduled. I had told him about the testimony of how God had provided for the tickets and visa and that it was all I had. I don't know where he found it, but within a short time, he had money for gas. We drove for about an hour and a half from Kampala to the place where the services were to be held. I had been informed that they had required security for me because of the Muslims, Satanists, and witch doctors in the area; and with me being an American Christian, it was not considered very safe for me. I was told I was to be off the compound by nine each night for my safety.

It also seemed like things weren't organized very well for the meetings for the day, but I just tried to go along with it. After I had been at the area where we were holding the open-air conference for a couple of days, the pastor from Kenya who was accompanying me was supposed to be arriving. The host pastor handed me his phone and told me I needed to call the pastor and tell him that when he arrived in Kampala, he needed to call that number. I did, but he lost it and called the number he had been using previously. They told him that they were no longer working with the pastor and gave him the right number to contact. When he arrived, he said, "I don't know what is going on, but these aren't the people we were working with for the conference."

During the day, they would have us pray for people; and then during the late afternoon, we would have our regular service with praise and worship and sharing of the Word. They were so watchful of me that if I got up to go to the bathroom in the night, someone was walking me out to the washroom and stood guard until I was through and would walk me back to the house.

I was amazed at the crowds that were there. I have never liked crowds, but I was able to be in front of that huge crowd and felt at total peace. It was a large compound, and the people would be crowded into the area, the tents around the outside were full, and there were people crowded on the balconies in the buildings around the compound. I was blown away with the size of the crowds. God had given me some prophecies on some numbers, and it turned out one was a date that the people in authority had literally made a pact causing the people to go into poverty. The pastors and a couple members of Parliament who were there gathered on the stage, asked for forgiveness for the wrongs they had done to the people, and prayed for God to forgive them. It was so powerful.

During the services, we saw God deliver a number of people from demon possession. We saw so many healing and salvation that I lost track of them all. It was so exciting to see God move. A couple I remember so vividly were a young mother who brought her daughter up to be prayed for healing of her legs. She had trouble walking and couldn't run. I stepped down from the platform to pray for her just to see all the security surround us. When they realized I was safe, they just kept a close eye on us. When we quit praying, the little girl could walk well but was still having trouble running. In the night, the Lord told me that the reason she was having trouble running was that she wasn't bending her knees; and if she would learn how to bend her knees, the problem would be resolved. She didn't come back the next night, and I have often wondered about her.

The other one came in the daytime for the morning prayers. She was always so sharply dressed, and I sensed she had been a professional woman at one time. She was in a flood and was holding on, trying to not be whisked away. The waters overpowered her, and in the process, all her lower teeth were broken off, and the teeth cut through her lower lip. It had not been sewn back together, so there was a gaping hole in her lip, and it was obvious she was very self-conscious about it. The first day she came for prayer, she told me her story through an interpreter. She wanted prayer for the pain she still had from the accident. We prayed for her, and the next day, she came saying the pain was gone, but she was having problems with her body trembling and wanted us to pray for the trembling to stop. We prayed against the trauma, and the trembling stopped.

The last day as they were ushering me off to the car to leave, I turned slightly. I could see her fighting through the crowd to try to get to me. I turned and reached around the ones between us and kissed her on the forehead before they got me into the car. I have thought of her so often and wondered what has happened to her. I pray for her that God would completely heal her mouth and restore her teeth. I know He can do it.

I realized that the host pastor had a very strong Jezebel spirit and seemed to always be manipulating things to continually get things the way he wanted them.

They had an orphanage and wanted me to take responsibility for raising funds for it. I told him I could give him organizations in the United States that do things like that, but to qualify, they would require accountability. He got upset, saying I was accusing him of stealing. I tried explaining I wasn't accusing him of anything; I was just telling him how it is for things like that in the United States. He had an administrative assistant who was very wise and asked to meet with us, wanting an explanation, which we had no problem doing.

I had set a budget I wanted to raise, but God prevented me from raising the amount. I was really disappointed and wondered what was going on. I had wanted to purchase a cow for the orphanage so they could have milk, but the funds didn't come in for anything but the flight and visa. The pastor who partnered with me understood the language some but not completely. The pastors would take up an offering for us and give it to the host pastor, but we never received it. He wanted me to go out with him to a ranch where cattle were raised. The owner wasn't there, and I felt God was protecting me. We tried to offer some solutions for helping the orphanage, but he always had an excuse for not wanting to check them out, and the main one was that someone else would be having responsibility for the funds, or he would have to be accountable to someone for his actions.

I did bring some jewelry that the girls had made to try to sell in the States. I was able to sell some of it but ended up purchasing the rest of what I couldn't sell so I could get the money to them. I was trying to get the funds to them, but I could not find anywhere that would let me send funds to Uganda because of so much scamming going on. I told them I knew the people it was going to, but that didn't make any difference.

I had chatted with the people we were originally working with, and even though they didn't go into a lot of detail, they did admit he was not a person to be trusted. They offered to let me send the money to them even though they really didn't want to deal with him. I told them I really didn't want to get them involved. I was finally able to send the money through Walmart, and by then, I also realized I needed to send it to the administrative assistant so there would be someone to verify that the money had been received.

That pastor gave me problems for better than six months. I had gotten to the point that I carbon-copied any correspondence to him to his administrative assistant. God would tell me when and how I was to respond to his letters. The day I was to go to my spiritual father's memorial service, I received a message asking what was going on between the pastor and me. I responded that it was between him and me and that I was not bringing this pastor into it. God has promised us that what the devil means for evil He will return for good. I knew he was trying to destroy me, but I received many invitations to minister from him, trying to destroy me. It really blew my mind as I could not see how any good could come from what he was trying to do, *but* God had a different plan.

I did maintain contact with some of the girls and the housemother for a while and am still in contact with the administrative assistant. I was told the pastor took many of the girls and the housemother from the orphanage and left them. It was so heartbreaking as the property that the orphanage was on had been the housemother's, but she had been persuaded to sign it over to him for the orphanage. She had given everything to him and lost it all. She tried to take care of the girls, but her health was not good, and she finally had to give it up. She has since passed on, but before she did, she told me they had never heard of the Jezebel spirit until I came along; and after I had opened their eyes to it, an evangelist came preaching about the Jezebel spirit, and revival was breaking out. I was so excited to hear it. Once again, the scripture fulfilled that one plants, another waters, and another harvests, but God brings the increase.

One of the girls whom the pastor has kept with him occasionally will send me a message asking how I am doing but never responds when I reply. I think of her often and pray for God to protect her and keep His hand on her. She was such a beautiful young lady and had such a sweet spirit.

We continued the trip down into Kenya. I had planned to help the place I had committed to come to with the expenses. I did not have the amount I had planned, so when I met up with the pastor at the bus station, I told him what we were dealing with. He chose to continue, and we would just walk in faith together. We had services every day except one for the whole time I was there. We went out into areas where many had not even seen a white person. The orphanages would be off the road, but when they would see the car coming with me in it, the children would come running out to greet me. We did stop at one and took pictures with the children. They were so excited. I think there must have been about fifty children at that facility. While ministering with that pastor, we saw many salvations and healings. I always get so excited seeing God work and so humbled to think that He has chosen to use me.

We went onto Nairobi, and I stayed with a friend there. Since we were out of funds, I joined another friend, and we attended many prayer services in the city for God to pour out His Spirit in revival on the country.

As usual, when you step out and do something like that in faith, you always have your people who will try to convince you that you haven't heard from God. Satan does not like it when you step out in faith like that and will do everything he can to discourage you. Since while I was gone I did not have any income from my job, the comeback was really difficult financially. God is always faithful as people worked with me to catch up with the bills. As far as the ones saying I hadn't heard from God, complete strangers would be prophesying over me and would confirm that I had; and because I had stepped out in faith and trusted Him, He would be using me to do more for the nations. God is always so faithful to not only honor His Word but to also honor those who are willing to step out and do what He has called us to.

In one of the trips, I had a reservation that was requiring that I change airports in France. I asked the agent a couple of times if I would be able to make the connection as there were only two hours between connecting flights. They kept confirming to me there would be no problem. I got to France and tried to get off the plane as quickly as I could. I went to the bathroom and went down to grab my bags. Since I had to change carriers, we weren't able to register the bags clear through. My bags were the first on the belt, so I grabbed them and headed to the door for the shuttle. All of a sudden, police and military with automatic rifles came running through the door as there was a terrorist alert. I continued to the door, stopping to make sure I had the right door. I got out to the shuttle to be informed I had missed my plane. I do admit I hadn't looked at a clock, but I do know I didn't take two hours. I said they had to be kidding, but they gave me directions on where to go to try to get the problem resolved.

I went into the ticket booth and was informed the information was correct, and I would have to spend two days there and purchase another ticket. I could not believe my boldness, and I knew it was God. I told them it was not acceptable. I was to be speaking at a conference in two days, and I didn't have money for another ticket. Had it been because of my negligence, I would understand; but where I had asked and been assured I could make the connection, then I shouldn't be held responsible.

I finally raised enough cain about it, and the agent said she would call a taxi to get me to the other airport. The taxi finally showed up and was told to hurry and get me over there. It was a typical traffic situation. He would change into the faster lane, which would almost stop. I quickly realized the taxi driver did not speak English and also that this was an attack of the enemy. I sent a text message back, requesting prayer for favor. I was laughing internally as I didn't want the taxi driver to think I was laughing at him. I judged he was around thirty-five years old and either Iranian or Basque. I was also laughing at the fact they had told him to hurry when I had already missed my flight since it wasn't going to get me there in time to catch it.

We got to the airport, and he was having problems making me understand what he wanted, but he was finally able to get me to understand. He loaded my luggage onto the cart and started running to the ticket booth. Later, I also laughed at how funny that must have looked with this young man running through the airport with this sixty-plus woman behind him. We got to the booth, and he started talking to the agent in the line to be informed that the line had just closed, and we would have to wait our turn. I could see his frustration, so I motioned to him to go ahead because I thought I could take care of it from there. While I was waiting, another man came up, also headed to Kenya from a different country, and said the same thing had happened to him.

My turn came, and I told the agent what was going on and once again enforced the fact I could not wait two days for the next flight. She asked me to wait a few minutes to see what she could do. Pretty soon she came back asking if I minded going to Kenya by way of Amsterdam. I replied I didn't care how I got there; I just needed to get there. She said it would be a ten-hour wait, but she could get me on that flight. I told her I would take it. The man I met said he would help me as he was familiar with that terminal and was amused that Abraham met Jacob at the airport in France.

Trying to get my luggage through seemed to be another challenge. I couldn't get the machine to work for me. I would try to ask for help, and it was just as though I was invisible, or there was a barrier that they could not hear my voice. Abraham came back to see how I was doing, and I told him. Finally, I was able to get someone to help me, but then they decided my carry-on bag wasn't allowed with my original ticket, and they were saying my personal bag was too heavy. They wanted me to pay another $210. I told them I didn't have it and asked for favor. I sensed God was telling me to trust Him, so I went and found a place close to Abraham and sat for a while. I had to go to the bathroom, and with the airport being under a terrorist alert, Abraham said I needed to take my bags with me.

I was coming out of the restroom when I ran into the person who had told me I needed to register my other bag, and she informed me if they wouldn't accept it, then they wouldn't let me on the plane, and I would miss my flight again. It frightened me, so I started the search all over again. I got in a line and was praying for God to give me favor. My turn came, and the agent gave me a lecture about not checking to see how the baggage regulations changed at different airports in different countries. I was fighting tears, but when he got through, I told him, "If the clothes in the big bags were for me, then it wouldn't be a concern, but all the things in the big bags were for the orphans. The clothes that I was taking for myself were in the carry-on bag and my personal bag. Could you please give me favor?" He started printing the labels, and I told him I didn't have the money to pay for them. He said he wasn't charging me for them.

I went back and told Abraham of how God had given me favor. Abraham disappeared on me, and when it came close to time to load, I headed to the gate for loading. He had told me we had the same flight, and I found him in a line to board. We talked a little, and I went onto my section. He said he would see me when we loaded. I never saw him again.

When I went to board, they were taking all carry-on luggage at no cost as they had the extra space. I realized how Satan had used the woman to cause me to doubt. If I had just listened to God instead of letting her put fear in my heart, I could have saved myself a lot of stress. He had already taken care of it, but I had to get in the flesh and let fear come in.

I boarded the plane and was sitting next to a woman from Morocco headed to Kenya. I explained to her my situation and told her I wasn't familiar with the Amsterdam airport, and I knew I didn't have much time to make the connecting flight. She said she was going to the same gate and suggested for me to stay with her. She said she would get me to where I needed to be. I stayed really close to her, and we got to the gate just as they were loading. She informed me which gate I was to take and said she had to board on the next gate. She totally disappeared.

I realized I had just entertained angels that I had not been aware of. God had sent His angels to guide me, protect me, and help me get to where I needed. I was reminded of the scripture once again in Psalm 34:7 (KJV): "The angel of the Lord encampeth round about them that fear him, and delivereth them." Psalms 91:11 (KJV) says, "For he shall give his angels charge over thee, to keep thee in all thy ways." And Hebrews 13:2 (KJV) states, "Be not forgetful to entertain strangers for thereby some have entertained angels unawares."

I was finally able to arrive in Kenya and was thankful to God for His protection, direction, and provision. I was exhausted and scheduled to be at the conference that night. My adopted son was the one who was scheduled to minister at all the open-air services. During the conference, I was to stay at the conference center a short distance away and then would be moving to the pastor's home when the conference was over.

After one of the outdoor services, my adopted African son came into the office while they were preparing for the next service. He had ministered, and I could tell he had poured his heart out even though the message wasn't in English. He buried his head in my neck and just wept. I just held him, and then God gave me a message for him. He had such an anointing of God that revival was going to pour out in his church. A couple of weeks later, he contacted me saying, in that Sunday morning service, the Spirit came down so powerfully that the praise and worship just kept going on. Finally, feeling like they needed to get on with the service, he moved the praise and worship team into his office. The Spirit kept falling and went around the walls of the church. He decided to just let God do what He wanted, and they had a wonderful service with the presence of God and no preaching. I felt like that was what God wanted for his church.

The hunger people had for God amazed me. People would come and be delivered from demon possession. While they were being delivered, they would be on the dirt floor; they would get up many times with mud covering their clothes. Sometimes they would stay through the whole service. If they lived close enough, they would go home, clean up, change clothes, come back, and enjoy the presence of God.

The people at the conference center were so good to me and very protective. The host pastor would send someone over to pick me up as he was too busy to come get me himself. If they hadn't seen them at the conference center with me, they wouldn't let them come up to get me. I know it was a frustration to the host pastor, but it was good to know that they were that protective of me. What was interesting was, when I had been in Kenya before, I had gone to their church with a friend where we would join them in interceding for Kenya over their lunch hour.

The pastor of the conference center and I had many long talks. He and his wife became such dear people to me. He wants me to minister at his church, but the doors haven't opened for me yet. I had told him about my experience in Uganda, and he said not a good thing comes from that country. I told him I disagreed as he was from there, and he was a good thing. I knew he was joking as we both know good people from that country. He would also tell me that the reason I had problems with the trips to Africa was that the devil didn't like me in Kenya as I did too much damage to his kingdom. I have never felt like I have done that much; I just try to do what God has called me to do and say what He wants me to say. I am glad it is doing damage in the devil's kingdom, though, and I give all the glory to God.

One time over there, I was at a conference, and one of the female pastors seemed to want my attention. I didn't feel really comfortable with her but prayed for my protection and stayed there talking with her until God opened the door so I could politely exit. I am always so amazed that if you let people go on long enough, if they are doing Satan's work, they will always expose themselves. As she was talking, she said she had prayed that Kenya would not get rain. They were suffering drought at the time, and after she confessed that, God gave me the open door to politely exit. I was sensing in my spirit that it wasn't of God, but I have also learned you don't want to start confronting territorial spirits that you don't have authority over without knowing it is being directed by God.

She ministered in the afternoon session, and I kept beating up myself as it seemed like her message was never going to end. It felt like she had ministered for two hours when she announced the scripture. I kept telling myself it was because it was in Swahili, but I had dealt with that before and never had this kind of problem. I just kept sensing something wasn't right.

That evening, one of the ministers felt God was saying he was to honor her, so he asked her to come forward. As he started honoring her, she started manifesting. She never would let the pastors or their wives pray her through deliverance. It broke my heart to see someone who was a minister of the gospel wanting to cling to her demons. This also helped me feel released for praying for the rain.

As I sought God, I felt God gave me the go-ahead to start taking authority and calling forth the rain. Since they had a lot of trouble with flooding, I was praying very specifically that the rain would be gentle so it would soak into the ground and not cause flooding but would be enough to turn the drought. After four days of praying, the rain started coming just as I had prayed. We had rain every single night or day until I left, and it was a nice gentle rain.

After a couple of days of rain, I started getting emails asking me to pray for the rain to stop. Most of the churches were poor and had holes in the roofs, so water was coming in and destroying what they had; also, many had dirt floors, so it was making it difficult to have church with the mud. I encouraged them to pray creatively that God would put an umbrella over their churches so the rain wouldn't go inside or pray for it not to rain where their church was sitting. Then

I asked them to pray for God to provide the funds when the rain stopped so they could repair the roof or get concrete poured for the floor.

I am amazed that God can take someone like me and use me the way He has. I wish I could share in this book all the things He has done, but there are so many things that I am trying to just touch on, hoping to encourage someone who is going through some hard struggles to not give up. God has a plan for you, and as you stay faithful, you will see that plan manifested, and it will bring you great peace and joy as you walk in His calling for your life.

I had planned on ending at this point, but God told me I was to write a sequel on my five months in Africa due to the COVID-19 pandemic. With the things that happened and the things God did during that time. There is another small book that could be written of what he did during that time.

Lightning Source UK Ltd.
Milton Keynes UK
UKHW041231160421
382072UK00008BA/455/J